ROCKY MOUNTAINS

by HERBERT S. ZIM, Ph.D., Sc.D.

in consultation with the

UNIVERSITY OF COLORADO MUSEUM STAFF
Boulder, Colorado

ILLUSTRATIONS BY
SU ZAN NOGUCHI SWAIN

 GOLDEN PRESS • NEW YORK
Western Publishing Company, Inc.
Racine, Wisconsin

FOREWORD

This Golden Guide attempts to introduce and explore a widely known region—big, varied, and open enough to tempt a multitude of visitors, many of whom stay to swell the fast-growing population. The high, cool mountains have a long and involved geologic history and a wealth of rocks, ores, and minerals. The climate they help create belies the summer heat and produces a richness and a variety of plant and animal life which all may enjoy.

Without the expert knowledge of Hugo Rodeck and his staff the selection and checking of data would have been difficult if not impossible. Richard Beidleman of Colorado College also made his wide field experience available. May I thank Gordon Alexander, William C. Bradley, John B. Chronic, Don Eff, Gladys R. Gary, Russell M. Honea, Edna Johnson, Albert Knorr, Urless N. Lanham, T. Paul Maslin, Clarence J. McCoy, John Rohner, Omer Stewart, Lowell E. Swenson, William A. Weber and Joe Ben Wheat of the University of Colorado Museum; also Robert P. Allen, H. Raymond Gregg, Arnold B. Grobman, Donald F. Hoffmeister, and Alexander Sprunt IV. Thanks go, also, to the artist, Su Zan Noguchi Swain, to Sonia Bleeker Zim for her work on the Indian tribes, and to all those who provided photographs.

H. S. Z

CONTENTS

3

JASPER NAT. PARK

BANFF NAT. PARK

Lake Louise   Calgary

ALBERTA

SASKATCHEWAN

South Saskatchewan R.

2

3

GLACIER NAT. PARK

MT. REVELSTOKE NAT. PARK

1

YOHO NAT. PARK

KOOTENAI NAT. PARK

BRITISH COLUMBIA

GLACIER-WATERTON INT'L. PEACE PARK

Fort Peck Res.

2

89   91

Missouri R.

87

M O N T A N A

93   Helena

Spokane

90

WASHINGTON

2

10

BIG HOLE BATTLEFIELD NAT. MON.

10   10

Snake R.

Columbia R.

95

YELLOWSTONE NAT. PARK

91

89

GRAND TETON NAT. PARK

I D A H O

30

OREGON

20   30

Boise

Snake R.

91

309

THE ROCKY MOUNTAIN REGION of this book is an arbitrary area of some 400,000 square miles, encompassing the core of the Rockies. Its 2,200-mile length includes parts of 5 states and 2 provinces. Large areas are still wild and unsettled. Check locally before heading back country on unpaved mountain roads.

93

Great Salt Lake

40

Salt

N E V A D A

40

50

95

HERE ARE THE ROCKIES

The Rocky Mountains form a 5,000-mile jagged backbone for North America from Mexico to Alaska. More than a hundred north-south ranges make up this mountain complex which reaches its greatest width (300 miles) in Colorado and Utah. Colorado alone boasts of 54 peaks over 14,000 ft. high. Mt. Elbert in Colorado reaches up to 14,419 feet but this falls far short of Alaska's Mt. McKinley, 20,320 ft.

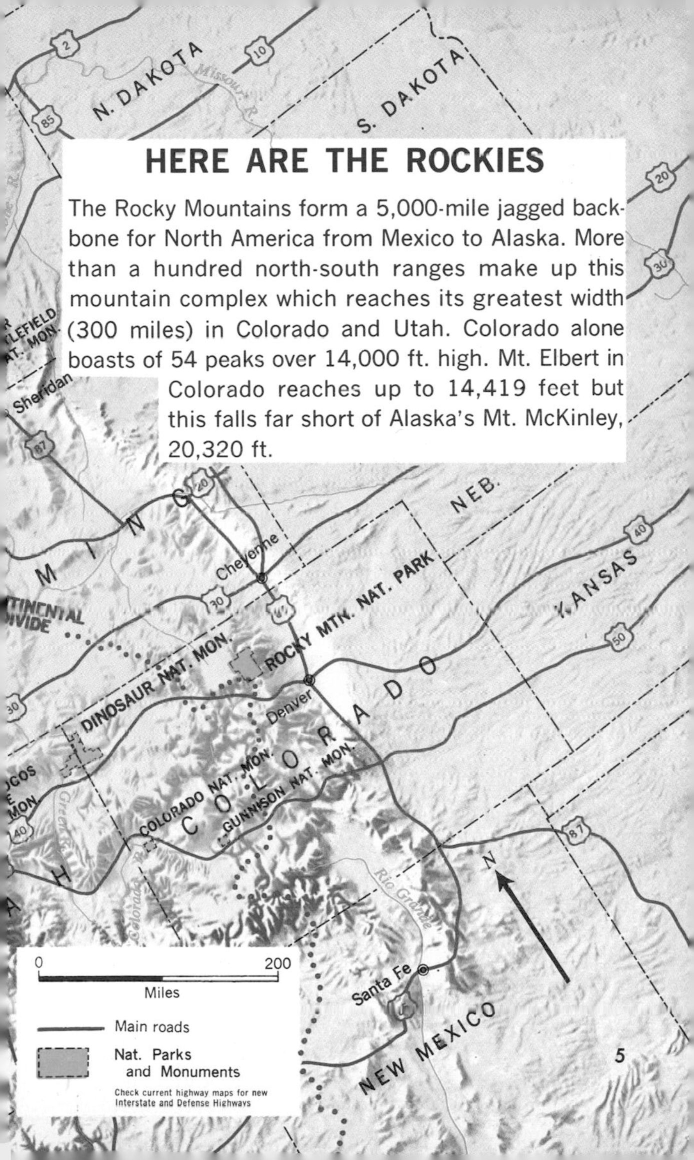

0   200
Miles

——— Main roads

Nat. Parks
and Monuments

Check current highway maps for new
Interstate and Defense Highways

5

The Rockies are not all mountainous. Between and around the snow-capped ranges and conifer-covered slopes are natural parklands, extensive plateaus, brush-covered flats and semi-arid deserts. Huge ranches and farmlands hug the mountains where land has been cleared and water made available.

At first a grim barrier to continental conquest, the Rockies gradually began to attract settlers because of furs, minerals, forests and agricultural land found there. Later, people came because of the stimulating climate and superb scenery. The Rocky Mountain region, still frontier country at the turn of the century, is now booming in population, industrial development and cultural growth. Vacationers and new residents join the old-timers in enjoying the freedom and exhilaration "out where the West begins."

Upturned edges of sandstone layers have eroded into unusual shapes; near Colorado Springs, Colorado

Simpkins—National Audubon Society

Hereford cattle pasture at the foot of the Sawtooth Mountains near Stanley, Idaho

The great Rocky Mountain system is often divided into a northern and a southern part, which are separated by broken plateaus extending from the Wyoming Basin to the Snake River Plain. The Northern Rockies begin north and west of Yellowstone National Park and extend on northwestward into Canada and Alaska.

The Southern Rockies are mainly long, uplifted ridges which, in rising, have upturned layers of sediments on either side. In the north the Rockies are more massive and do not form ridges with upturned foothills. In both areas the Rockies form the Continental Divide, where the slopes turn rain and melting snow into either the Atlantic or the Pacific drainage. The Divide and most Rocky ranges are crossed by mountain passes (the lowest usable paths across the mountains), through which roads and railroads funnel at elevations between 7,500 and 12,000 ft. The discovery of South Pass in 1812 and others afterward hastened the opening of the West. Colorado has 136 named passes, and the total number for the Rockies may approach 500.

In general, mountain soil is poor and rocky but in the natural basins or parks are rich grasslands. On the flanks of the Rockies—especially to the east and in river valleys —the soil is good and, with irrigation, produces fine crops. Irrigation means that corn, alfalfa, melons, sugar beets and truck crops can be raised. Without irrigation, dry farming may produce sorghum, wheat, corn or enough grass for pasture. What used to be open range is now fenced and improved for cattle. Sheep make the most of thinner mountain pastures.

The water of mountain streams and lakes is carried by ingenious tunnels and ditches to supply power and irrigation needs. Other natural resources of the Rockies include great forests of pine, spruce and fir with some hardwoods at lower levels. The geologic activity that followed the uplift of the mountains honeycombed the country rock with veins rich in lead, zinc, silver, gold and copper. Petroleum has been discovered in the Wyoming basins and elsewhere. Coal is mined in the Rocky Mountain foothills.

The exploitation of these natural resources and the region's climate and geographic position have created industries which bolster the mountain economy. Rapid transportation by rail and air, plus the security of the inland area, make the region attractive to new atomic and electronic industries as well as to heavy and light manufacturing. The region is far less dependent upon eastern manufacturing than it was a generation ago.

The tourist and visitor are attracted by what might be considered lesser natural resources. But the combination of climate, scenery and a richness of native plants and animals expresses the unique physical and biologic factors that unite to make this region so outstanding. Besides, the Rockies are more centrally located than one might believe. Denver, the gateway to the Rockies, is 830 air miles from Los Angeles, 910 from Chicago, 1,460 from Washington, 1,200 from Atlanta, 1,020 from Seattle, and 1,080 from New Orleans.

Rich farms fill the river valleys near Missoula, Montana

Bob and Ira Spring

ROCKY MOUNTAIN CLIMATE is affected by altitude, latitude and geography. Temperature falls about 3½°F. with every thousand feet of climb and drops about 1½° as one moves north one degree of latitude (about 66 miles). Daytime summer temperatures may be warm or hot, but nights are cool. In mountain valleys, winter temperatures may drop to −60°F. but the low humidity helps modify the effect of both heat and cold. Snow may be heavy through spring and may persist in the mountains all summer. Western slopes get the most moisture. The eastern "rain shadow" may get as little as ten inches a year. Skies are cloudless or nearly so, with some summer thunderstorms. In winter the unusual chinook winds blow down the east slopes, raising the temperature markedly in just a few hours.

CLIMATIC DATA FOR SOME ROCKY MOUNTAIN CITIES

City	Altitude	Latitude	Slope E. or W.	Avg. Jan. temp.	Avg. July temp.	Annual precip.
Banff, Alberta	4,538 ft.	51°N	East	13°F	57°F	21 in.
Calgary, Alberta	3,439 ft.	51°N	East	18°F	75°F	17 in.
Missoula, Mont.	3,223 ft.	47°N	West	22°F	68°F	14 in.
Helena, Mont.	4,047 ft.	47°N	East	20°F	66°F	13 in.
Butte, Mont.	5,716 ft.	46°N	West	23°F	65°F	14 in.
W. Yellowstone, Mont.	6,667 ft.	45°N	East	13°F	58°F	19 in.
Rapid City, S.D.	3,229 ft.	44°N	East	23°F	72°F	18 in.
Sun Valley, Idaho	6,000 ft.	44°N	West	31°F	82°F	18 in.
Boise, Idaho	2,842 ft.	44°N	West	27°F	75°F	11 in.
Casper, Wyo.	5,123 ft.	43°N	East	26°F	72°F	15 in.
Pocatello, Idaho	4,461 ft.	43°N	West	26°F	72°F	13 in.
Rock Springs, Wyo.	6,271 ft.	42°N	West	19°F	69°F	7 in.
Cheyenne, Wyo.	6,060 ft.	41°N	East	27°F	67°F	16 in.
Salt Lake City, Utah	4,390 ft.	40°N	West	30°F	77°F	16 in.
Vernal, Utah	5,050 ft.	40°N	West	17°F	70°F	9 in.
Denver, Colo.	5,280 ft.	40°N	East	32°F	73°F	14 in.
Leadville, Colo.	10,188 ft.	39°N	East	18°F	56°F	20 in.
Colorado Spr., Colo.	5,900 ft.	39°N	East	30°F	68°F	14 in.
Gunnison, Colo.	7,681 ft.	39°N	West	8°F	61°F	10 in.

Changes in life zones are evident in the Seven Devils Range, Idaho. Conifers thin out at higher altitudes

LIFE ZONES include communities of plants and animals which, in turn, reflect the relationship between climate and altitude. Each thousand feet up the Rockies brings a temperature drop equal to a 200-mile journey north. Since temperature and rainfall often determine the kind of plants that will survive, typical communities develop in areas that have a common local climate. Thus, as one climbs the Rockies, the changes he sees in plant and animal life reflect the same changes he would see if he had traveled north.

The plant communities and the life zones they form are not clear cut. The western side of the Rockies has more rainfall than the eastern slopes and this makes for richer plant life. The Rockies, as covered in this book, extend over 2,000 miles north and south, so the average temper-

11

atures run some 20° less in the Canadian Rockies than in central Colorado. In Colorado, one must climb to 11,500 feet to reach the timberline, the point above which no trees grow. The timberline is at about 9,000 feet in Montana and at only 7,000 feet in northern Alberta.

Spring tends to come about one day later and fall one day earlier for every 100-ft. rise in elevation. This makes summer at the Colorado timberline only about six weeks long—from July to mid-August. The tiny alpine flowers growing in mats and cushions (pp. 62–63) burst into bloom all at once and are soon gone. Birds at timberline nest later and migrate earlier than those on the Plains.

Below is a chart of the generalized life zones for the Rockies of Colorado. Farther north the warm Sonoran Zone disappears and the other zones are at lower levels. In much of the Rockies the Transition and Canadian zones fuse and overlap. The treatment of flowers, shrubs, trees, mammals and birds (pp. 62–107) generally follows a zonal pattern which will both help one to recognize life zones and make identification easier.

LIFE ZONES IN THE ROCKIES

Zone	Location	Elevation	Typical plants
Arctic-Alpine	above timberline	over 11,500 ft.	Alpine grasses, lichens, sedges, Dwarf Willow
Hudsonian	high mountains to timberline	11,500 10,000	Limber Pine, Engelmann Spruce, Bristlecone Pine
Canadian	lower mountains	10,000 8,000	Quaking Aspen, Lodgepole Pine, Douglas Fir, Ponderosa Pine
Transition	foothills	8,000 6,000	Piñon Pine, oaks, Rocky Mt. Juniper
Upper Sonoran		6,000 4,500	Cottonwood, willows, Box Elder, Sagebrush

A variety of accommodations are available for visitors in the Rockies; this is a chalet in Glacier National Park

THE VISITOR comes to the Rockies with a parcel of clear expectations. He will not be disappointed. The summer climate is stimulating and the cool nights are restful. The scenery is unrivaled. Activities range from dude ranching, hunting, fishing and camping down to plain, unadulterated relaxation. Enjoy the Rockies to the fullest, but come prepared. Remember, it takes a bit of time to get acclimated to altitudes over 7,000 ft. Avoid exertion the first few days. Wear appropriate, comfortable clothing and have warm jackets or sweaters for the cool evenings. Sturdy shoes make walking a pleasure. Don't be deceived by distances on a road map. Mountain driving requires care and should be done slowly. Stop often to enjoy the scenery and to relax. Check before taking ungraded mountain roads or local short cuts. In summer there may be mosquitoes along lakes and streams and biting flies in the forests. Ticks occur in grasslands and brushland. Some ticks are carriers of disease. Rattlers are found but not commonly in the mountains. Leave them alone. In short, take the same care out-of-doors that you would at home.

13

MORE INFORMATION on the Rockies may be had from federal and state sources.

National Forests: U.S. Forest Service, *for E. Wyo. and Colo.,* Federal Center, Denver 2, Colo. *For W. Wyo., Utah and S. Idaho,* Forest Service Bldg., Ogden, Utah. *For N. Idaho, Mont.,* Federal Bldg., Missoula, Mont.

National Parks and Monuments: National Park Service, Washington 25, D.C., or the regional office for the Rockies, National Park Service, Omaha 2, Nebraska.

COLORADO   Adv. and Publicity Dept., Capitol Bldg., Denver 2
WYOMING   Travel Comm., State Ofc. Bldg., Cheyenne
IDAHO   State Dept. of Commerce & Dev., Capitol Bldg., Boise
MONTANA   Travel and Adv. Dept., State Highway Comm., Helena
UTAH   Road and Tourist Info., State Capitol Bldg., Salt Lake City
BRITISH COLUMBIA   Gov't Travel Bureau, Parliament Bldg., Victoria, B.C.
ALBERTA   Gov't Travel Bureau, Legislative Bldg., Edmonton, Alberta

MAPS are essential. Use road maps from several sources, especially to check minor roads. Detailed topographic maps are fine for hikers. Write U.S. Geological Survey, Washington 25, D.C., for a free key map of each state you desire and for order forms.

BOOKS on this region are plentiful. Most deal with specific subjects, such as history, mining, trees, or birds. Below are some guides and general introductions. Those of the W.P.A. Writers' Project tend to be dated but still have a wealth of pertinent detail.

Colorado   Ormes, Robert M., GUIDE TO COLORADO MOUNTAINS, Sage, 1955 Writers' Project, COLORADO, Rev. Ed., 1951, Hastings.
Wyoming   Bonney, O. H. and L., GUIDE TO THE WYOMING MOUNTAINS AND WILDERNESS AREAS, 1960, Sage. Writers' Project, WYOMING, GUIDE TO ITS HISTORY, HIGHWAYS AND PEOPLE, 1941, Oxford Univ. Press.
Idaho   Writers' Project, IDAHO, A GUIDE IN WORD AND PICTURE, 1950, Oxford Univ. Press.
Montana   Writers' Project, MONTANA, Rev. Ed., 1955, Hastings. Howard, Joseph K., MONTANA, HIGH, WIDE AND HANDSOME, Rev. Ed., 1959, Yale.
Utah   Writers' Project, UTAH, Rev. Ed., 1954, Hastings.
British Columbia   Goodchild, Fred H., BRITISH COLUMBIA, ITS HISTORY, PEOPLE AND INDUSTRY, 1951, Macmillan. Ormsby, M. A., BRITISH COLUMBIA, 1958, Macmillan.

Denver's Civic Center, viewed from the dome of the State Capitol Building, is a symbol of the Rockies' growth

During the next decades centennials of all sorts will be celebrated up and down the Rockies. Colorado began in 1959 with the centennial of its gold rush. All these celebrations will serve as reminders of the prodigious growth of this region. Progress has not been steady. At the half-century point many mining booms had already burst. Towns were abandoned as the ores gave out. But the second half-century has seen a pronounced change. New dams and tunnels have made cheap power and irrigation water available. The airplane has supplemented roads and railroads to bring the Rockies within a few hours of both coasts. New heavy industry has stabilized the economy, and old standbys like cattle and sheep raising, lumber and farming have become more productive. New and bigger cities boast of schools, universities, parks, zoos and museums. As you pass through cities listed on the next three pages watch for worthwhile things to see and do.

15

The U.S. Air Force Academy, in the foothills just north of Colorado Springs

COLORADO

Denver: mile-high capital of, and largest city in, Colo. Established in 1860 by prospectors and miners in eastern shadow of Rockies. Growing commercial, agricultural and vacation center. Site of U.S. Mint, Air Force base and school, Univ. of Denver, colleges, museums, zoo, and many municipally owned mountain parks.

Colorado Springs: Resort city. Toll road and cog train to 14,110-ft. summit of Pikes Peak. Has broad streets, fine homes and parks; art center, Colo. College, Will Rogers Shrine, Garden of the Gods; Zoo; USAF Academy; home of N.A. Air Defense Command.

Pueblo: Steel plant, manufacturing center, irrigated valley area. State fair and rodeo.

Grand Junction: Nearby mineral deposits and irrigated farmlands. Gateway to Colo. Nat. Mon. Visit observatory in Grand Mesa Nat. Forest, which also has ski slopes and tows.

Boulder: Univ. of Colo. and Museum; Nat. Bureau of Standards lab. Winter sports, Chautauqua summer program; annual rodeo. Fine mountain parks and Flagstaff scenic highway.

Greeley: Agricultural marketing center established by famous editor of N.Y. *Tribune,* Horace Greeley. Colorado State College, Meeker Memorial Museum. USDA Experimental Station.

Fort Collins: Agricultural center and residential city, home of Colo. State Univ.; Pioneer Museum. Follow Route 14 west to Mountain Park and fish hatcheries.

MONTANA

Helena: Capital of Montana. Past and present linked with gold, silver and lead mining. Museum, art gallery, cathedral.

Butte: Extensive underground copper and zinc mines. Agricultural and stock center. School of Mines has fine museum.

Great Falls: Industrial and financial center—largest city in Montana. Art gallery, annual state fair and rodeo. Giant Springs and Lewis and Clark National Forest are nearby.

16

Bozeman: In rich agricultural and live-stock land of Gallatin Valley. Montana State College started here in 1893. Nearby is Gallatin Nat. Forest and the Gallatin Gateway of Yellowstone Nat. Park.

Livingston: Railroad center, timber industries. Scenic drive from here goes to Gardiner, entrance to Yellowstone Nat. Park.

Billings: Rail center, oil and sugar refineries. Historical museum, scenic drives. Headquarters for nearby Custer Nat. Forest. Annual rodeo.

Anaconda: Copper smelter. Nearby campgrounds, fishing, lakes and streams, dinosaur beds. Abundant wildlife in Pintlar Wilderness Area.

Missoula: Training school for Forest Service Smokejumpers. Livestock auctions, Montana State University. Fish, game and guides nearby.

Kalispell: Agricultural market center surrounded by recreation areas including Hungry Horse Dam, Glacier Nat. Park, Flathead Lake and Flathead Nat. Forest.

WYOMING

Casper: Center of sheep, cattle and oil region. Replica of Ft. Caspar. Nearby are Casper Mountain Park, Hell's Half Acre and Independence Rock.

Cheyenne: Home of world-famous Frontier Days in July; maintains Old West flavor throughout year. State's largest city and capital. Commercial, ranching and rail center surrounded by ranch country.

Laramie: Quiet western town between mountain ranges. Ranching and sportsmen's center. Site of University of Wyoming; fossil museum.

IDAHO

Idaho Falls: Idaho's second largest city, has waterfalls and picnic areas. Nearby lands irrigated by Snake River produce grain and potatoes. Atomic Energy Commission's national reactor testing station just west of city on Lost River Plains.

Pocatello: On Oregon Trail in broad valley of Snake River at western edge of Rockies. Trading, railroad and college center. Near giant American Falls Reservoir (irrigation and power) and historic site of Old Fort Hall.

UTAH

Salt Lake City: Capital of Utah. Near desert, Great Salt Lake and mountains. World headquarters of Mormon Church; famous for Mormon Tabernacle, choir, and temple. Largest city between Denver and West Coast. Agricultural, industrial, mining, especially copper, and cultural center. Museums, art collections, colleges and university.

Ogden: Important rail center and shipping point for livestock. Utah's second largest city. Lies between mountains and Great Salt Lake. Site of U.S. Forest Service experimental station. East through Ogden Canyon is Snow Basin winter sports area.

Provo: A cultural and steel center near rich agricultural land. Site of Mormon Brigham Young Univ. Nearby and to the north towers Mt. Timpanogos (12,008 ft.).

Logan: Site of Utah State Univ. Located on edge of historic and fertile Cache Valley. Logan Canyon leads northeast to Bear Lake.

ALBERTA

Calgary: Zoological and natural history park has models of dinosaurs. Site of fish hatchery, bird sanctuary, packing plants and flour mills. Gateway to Banff and Jasper Nat. Pks.

Lethbridge: Sugar beet refineries, vegetable canning and freezing plants. Visit large earth-filled dam on St. Mary's River and Waterton-Glacier International Peace Park.

BRITISH COLUMBIA

Revelstoke: First settled as a railroad center, now has farming, lumber and mining as chief industries. Mt. Revel-stoke Nat. Park headquarters are here. Located at junction of Columbia and Illecillewaet rivers.

Nelson: On west branch of Kootenay Lake; has complete tourist facilities. Nearby are ghost towns, old settlements and picnicking and sports areas.

Kimberley: Site of the famous Sullivan Mine, the world's largest producer of lead, zinc and silver. Tours.

Trail: In a narrow valley on the banks of the Columbia River. Public park, beaches, and outdoor theater. Tour the famous Cominco smelter (producing silver, lead and zinc) and its chemical fertilizer plant.

Spires of the Mormon Temple are a landmark in Salt Lake City

A family camps at 12,000 ft. near Continental Divide in Colorado

TOURING THE ROCKIES is more fun if you do some advance planning. Send for road maps, guide books and travel folders. Major oil companies offer free tour aid. Remember this is mountainous country—try to keep each day's travel well under 300 miles. Make reservations for hotels and resorts. Arrive early to get campsites during the busy summer season. Start your day early and stop early. This gives you more time for side trips, recreation, fishing or local sightseeing.

Best time for travel in the Rockies is late June to early September. Higher elevations may be snowbound into early July. Check tires and brakes before starting. Traffic, game and conservation laws vary, as do campsite costs, entrance and admission fees. Check in advance. Use your car's ash tray and a litter bag. Keep campsites clean. Try one of the following suggested tours or plan your own after checking the last section of this book (pp. 116–156).

TWO TOURS through the Rockies, each planned for one week, will give you a chance to see the northern or southern Rockies—or both. Both trips start from Yellowstone Park but you can pick them up at any place en route. The first tour, to the north, covers 1,700 miles in a week, but try to add a few extra days at Yellowstone at the beginning or the end, as your schedule permits.

1st day: From Gardiner via U.S. 89 and 10 to Three Forks, then north on Route 287 to Helena (capital and museums) to spend the night.

2nd day: Continue north on Route 287 to Browning; then circle south and west on U.S. 2 to West Glacier.

3rd day: Drive back east through Glacier N.P. to St. Mary; swing north on U.S. 89 and Canada 2 to Calgary, or use Routes 6 and 3 from Babb to visit Waterton Park en route.

4th day: Move from the plains back into the mountains via Route 1 to Banff. See Lake Louise and head west via 1A or 1B to Route 95. Take the 160-mile trip north to the Columbia Ice Field if you have an extra day. Spend the night at Radium Hot Springs on Route 95.

5th day: Head south on Route 95 to Cranbrook; then on 93 and cross the border. On to White Fish or Kalispell for the night.

6th day: Continue on 93 to Missoula and then on U.S. 10 to Anaconda. Visit the copper smelters.

7th day: Return on U.S. 10S and 10 to Bozeman and south on U.S. 191 to West Yellowstone. Here the park and road system connects to Gardiner and to roads east and south.

South trip is a bit shorter but has a greater east-west swing. Denver can be visited or by-passed depending on your feeling about big cities. The museums and parks are excellent.

1st day: From Yellowstone N.P. take U.S. 89 through Grand Teton N.P.; then via Montpelier and Logan Canyon to Ogden, Utah.

2nd day: Drive south through Salt Lake City on U.S. 91. Take cutoff to Timpanogos Cave N. Mon. Continue on to Heber, and swing east on U.S. 40 to Vernal.

3rd day: Continue east on U.S. 40, visiting Dinosaur N.M. Stay on 40, turning short of Granby onto U.S. 34 and Grand Lake.

4th day: Start early through Rocky Mountain N.P. over Trail Ridge Road to Estes Park. Take Routes 66 and 7 to Boulder (U. of Colo.); toll turnpike to Denver (capital, parks and museums) or take 119 as a cutoff. Push west on U.S. 6 to Dowds and south on U.S. 24 to Leadville.

5th day: Continue south and east on U.S. 24 via Buena Vista and Florissant to Colorado Springs. A side road takes you up Pikes Peak. See the Garden of the Gods and Air Force Academy, then on to Denver via the freeway.

6th day: Via U.S. 87 or 287 to Fort Collins, then on U.S. 287 to Laramie and Rawlins.

7th day: Continue on U.S. 287 to Lander, then turn east and north via 789 and 20 to Cody and on to east entrance of Yellowstone Nat. Park.

CALENDAR OF EVENTS

(Verify locally and check for specific dates)

January Nat. Western Livestock Show, Horse Show and Rodeo, Denver.

April Red Rock Park, Denver—and elsewhere—Easter Sunday sunrise services in natural amphitheaters.

May Cherry Blossom Festival, Canon City, Colo.; Sports Car Races, Memorial Day, La Junta, Colo.; Vigilante Parade and Mont. Institute of Arts Festival, Helena, Mont.; Gold Spike Festival, Ogden, Utah; Apple Blossom Festival, Fayette, Idaho (first week); Fishing Derby (May–Nov.), Sandpoint, Idaho; Log Drive Festival, Priest River, Idaho.

June Rodeos, Billings and Miles City, Montana; Indian Sun Dances at Montana reservations; State Mineral and Gem Show, Rock Springs, Wyo.; Pack Burro Race across Mosquito Pass, Leadville, Colo.; Central City Festival, Central City, Colo. (through Aug.); Horse Show and Rodeo, continues first week of July, Greeley, Colo.

July Summer season of cultural events and entertainment at Aspen, Central City, Denver, etc. Make local inquiry. Widespread July 4th rodeos, celebrations, festivities and speeches. Summer Chautauqua, Boulder, Colo. (through Aug.); Pow Wow Days, Rodeo (last week), Boulder; Rodeo and Pioneer celebration (2nd week), Canon City, Colo.; Cattlemen's Days Rodeo (3rd week), Gunnison, Colo.; Pioneer Day Rodeo (late July), Idaho Falls; Snake River Stampede, Nampa, Ida.; Frontier Days celebration, Cheyenne, Wyo.; Calgary Exhibition and Stampede (week following July 4); Pioneer Days, rodeos, parades, pageants (late July), Ogden, Utah; U. of Utah Music Festival (early July) and Days of '47 celebrations, Salt Lake City; Indian sun dances and ceremonies, Browning and Fort Belknap, Montana; Rodeos, Livingston, Red Lodge, Mont.; Wolf Point Stampede (mid-July), Wolf Point, Mont.

August Yacht Club Regatta, Grand Lake, Colo.; Kids' Rodeo, La Junta, Colo.; State Fair and Rodeo (late Aug. or early Sept.), Pueblo, Colo.; Pikes Peak or Bust Rodeo, Colo. Springs; All American Indian Days celebration (1st week), Sheridan, Wyo.; Gift of the Waters Indian Pageant (Hot Springs State Park), Thermopolis, Wyo.; Central Wyo. Fair and Night Rodeo (mid-Aug), Casper, Wyo.; Midland Empire Fair and Rodeo (mid-Aug.), Billings, Mont.; Northern Mont. State Fair and Rodeo (1st week), Great Falls, Mont.; Nat. Fresh Water Trout Derby, Festival of Nations, Livingston, Mont.; War Bonnet Roundup (mid-Aug.), Idaho Falls, Ida.

September Aspencade (guided tour of the high country—mid-Sept.), Steamboat Springs, Colo.; Utah State Fair, Salt Lake City, Utah; Peach Day (rodeo, wrestling, boxing), Brigham, Utah; N. W. Montana Fair and Rodeo, Kalispell, Mont.; State Fair and Rodeo, Douglas, Wyo.; Rodeo (Labor Day weekend), Thermopolis, Wyo.; National Steer Roping Finals, Laramie, Wyo.; Rodeo and Roundup (Labor Day weekend), Lewiston, Idaho.

November Livestock Show (mid-Nov.), Ogden, Utah.

Piute hunting camp

THE GOOD OLD DAYS

The Rockies were the homelands of numerous nomadic tribes, mainly hunters of buffalo, deer and elk. They included the Shoshoni, Ute and Piute, who also gathered edible roots and seeds. From about 1600 eastern tribes, pushed out of their lands by other Indians and, later, by white settlers, trekked to the High Plains and Rockies seeking new homes. Those who came prospered, for after 1700 most of the Indians acquired horses and began to enjoy a more abundant life. They could move faster, hunting buffalo, and covered longer distances when trading with neighboring tribes. Their basket-like shelters gave way to skin covered tipis which could be quickly taken down and moved. Tribes warred over hunting grounds and raided each other's camps for sheer glory and reckless adventure. Early contacts with Europeans were beneficial to the tribes, giving them trade goods and other new materials. This soon gave way to bloody conflicts and wars.

There are no written records of the original lands and

SARSI

ALBERTA

SASKATCHEWAN

† Old McDougall Mission

■ Fort Macleod

BLACKFOOT

FORT BELKNAP RES.

GROS

BRITISH COLUMBIA

KUTENAI

ROCKY BOY'S RES.

GROS VEN

BLACKFEET RES.

Flathead Lake

FLATHEAD RES.

MONT

KALISPEL

FLATHEAD

○ Helena

Fort Owen State Mon.

● Butte

WASHINGTON

COEUR D'ALENE

† Cataldo Mission

CLARK

● Big Hole Battlefield

○ Virginia City

LEWIS

AND

NEZ PERCE

Bannock Mon.

Chapel of Transfiguration

OREGON TRAIL

IDAHO

Columbia R.

OREGON

PIUTE

Fort Hall

FO

SHOSHON

(including BANN

Promontory Point

OVERLAND STAGE

Great Salt Lake

Salt

Bands of hunters remained within their tribal boundaries, except during raids and warfare. Bands that were isolated from the rest of the tribe might eventually use only their band name. This has led to confusion about tribal names and tribal boundaries.

■ Old forts

○ Early settlements

● Monuments and battlefields

† Missions

•••• Trails

0   200

Miles

---- Indian reservations

||||| Original tribal lands

N. DAKOTA

S. DAKOTA

SIN/BOIN

attlefield
Mon.
TONGUE
RIVER
RES.

Fetterman
Massacre

t Kearny

W

Y
O
M
I
N
G

SIOUX

WIND
RIVER
RES.

Fort Caspar

Mormon
Ferry

ependence Rock

ARAPAHO

OREGON TRAIL

Laramie

Fort Russell

Fort Sander

STAGE

Fort Collins

OVERLAND

rt Bridger

Central City

Denver

CHEYENNE

KANSAS

NEB.

Meeker

Leadville

Cripple Creek

Fort Lyon

C
O
L
O
R
A
D
O

TAH
and
OURAY
RES.

A
H

Green R.

U
T
E

Fort Garland

N

Colorado R.

Rio Grande

Santa Fe

NEW MEXICO

early migrations of these people before the coming of Europeans. By studying tribal kinship, religions, languages, myths and legends, anthropologists have pieced a good part of the story together. We thus know that the Crow, Blackfoot, Shoshoni, Ute and Piute occupied their lands for a much longer time than the relative newcomers, the Cheyenne, Arapaho, Sioux and Assiniboin. The Kutenai, newcomers also, were originally buffalo hunters who were pushed northward.

THE SHOSHONI, UTE, PIUTE AND BANNOCK lived in adjoining territories and spoke Uto-Aztecan languages that had a common origin. The total population of these tribes was estimated at 15,000, but the Indians lived in bands of a few families each. These bands wandered over the barren lands of the basins and plateaus, led by a chief who was an able hunter or an older man. While the men looked for game, the women and children gathered berries, nuts, and seeds, which they ground into meal. This was cooked in the handsome watertight baskets the women skillfully wove. A stew was boiled by dropping heated stones into it. These tribes lived in wickiups—homes built of poles and reeds, like huge woven baskets. For warmth they plastered the wickiups with mud mixed with grass. The women tanned deer and antelope skins for clothes and wove plant fibers to make skirts. They also wove strips of rabbit fur into warm robes and blankets.

This simple, isolated life changed after 1700. The Shoshoni were among the first to learn to breed horses in their sheltered valleys. They traded horses to the eager Plains hunters for buffalo robes, tipi covers, and tanned buckskins. Shoshoni traders lingered on the Plains to hunt and began to feud with the Blackfoot, the Cheyenne and Sioux over buffalo territory.

In 1805, a Shoshoni woman, Sacajawea, and her husband guided the Lewis and Clark Expedition across the Rockies, and introduced the explorers to her people. Thus peaceful relations with the whites began. After 1869, the Shoshoni and Bannock entered reservations at Ft. Hall, Lemhi and Wind River. Their chief, Washakie, said at the time that he was yielding to the "superior tools and terrible weapons of the whites."

26

Early photograph of Shoshone camp in Wyoming; the tent in the foreground is that of Chief Washakie

The Ute raided Spanish and Pueblo Indian settlements to the south and occasionally crossed the mountains to the Colorado Plains to hunt buffalo. After they got horses, the warlike Ute increased their raids. However, they later retired peacefully to reservations. A "war" flared up in 1879 because the Ute, already living on short government rations, were forced into farming—an occupation they considered unworthy of hunters and warriors. The uprising was quickly suppressed. Ironically, recent discovery of oil and uranium on their reservations has put the modern Ute among the wealthiest Indians.

The Piute, which may mean "true Ute," lived mainly as plant and seed gatherers, while the Bannock—a detached branch of the Northern Piute—became buffalo hunters. In 1860 the Piute clashed with gold prospectors. Later they were placed on reservations.

27

THE BLACKFOOT, one of the largest (estimated population 10,000) and most aggressive groups of northern buffalo hunters, roamed over a vast territory in Montana and Canada. Originally from the eastern woodlands, the Blackfoot were so named because of their moccasins, blackened by grass fires started to stampede the buffalo herds.

The Blackfoot were allies of the Blood Indians, Piegans, Atsina and Sarsi. Together they fought the Cree, Assiniboin, Shoshoni, Crow and Sioux. By 1750 the Blackfoot had horses; by 1770, guns. Then they and their allies raided south for more horses and, into the Rockies, for caches of furs, stored by the French and Indian trappers. Rich and powerful, the Blackfoot held religious ceremonies honoring the Great Manitou and Sun Dances to assure good buffalo hunting. They traded sacred bundles and songs with their allies to acquire greater hunting powers. They feasted and gambled and, at campfires, told tales of personal bravery and stories from their rich past.

The smallpox epidemics of 1836, 1845, and 1857 brought disaster to the Blackfoot. Their population was reduced by two thirds. Epidemics hit the neighboring tribes and decimated them too. Soon after, the buffalo began to disappear and by 1880, these frightened, demoralized people faced starvation. Both the United States and Canadian governments provided rations and clothing, and placed the Blackfoot on three small reservations in the United States and two in Alberta, Canada.

THE FLATHEAD, numbering about 3,000, were related to the Indians of the Northwest Coast, although the Bitterroot Valley of Montana was their original home. They never practiced flattening of infants' heads, but were so named in error by the French. The Flathead fought the

Louis Frohman—The New York Public Library

A summer camp of the Blackfoot gathered for buffalo hunting

Blackfoot for buffalo lands, but lost, and in the end were pressed northward. In 1855 they were placed on reserves near Flathead Lake, Montana, and in the Bitterroot Valley. Many had already been converted to Catholicism by Father de Smet. In 1872 part of the Bitterroot Valley Reserve was purchased from the Flathead and opened to white settlers.

THE KUTENAI, numbering only 1,000, were buffalo hunters in the early days. They were pushed northward from the Plains by the Siksika and Cree, who were allies of the Blackfoot. The hunting Kutenai continued to live in tipis. Those who became fishermen along Idaho and Canadian lakes built lodges of rushes and poles. They speared and trapped fish from bark canoes, made in an ancient style. The Kutenai worshiped the sun and believed their dead went there to live. Otherwise, their beliefs were like those of the Plains Indian hunters. In 1855 and 1867, the Kutenai were put on reservations in Montana and Idaho.

29

PLAINS INDIAN TRIBES, who lived along the east front of the Rockies, hunted in the mountain valleys. They were mainly buffalo hunters, though some of them farmed.

As tribes from the rich prairies were pushed into the High Plains, each spread over a territory which they later claimed and defended as their homeland. For all these newcomers to the Rockies, the buffalo became the mainstay of life, supplying food, clothing, and shelter. The horse made hunting and moving easier, and for over a century the Plains tribes prospered.

In the 1870's and 1880's as the buffalo disappeared, the tribes were defeated and forced to reservations. The Plains tribes living closest to the Rockies were:

THE CROW, who call themselves Absaroke (meaning Sparrowhawk, Crow or Bird People), were divided into western or Mountain Crow and eastern or River Crow. Their total population was about 4,000. Crow men were exceptional horsemen and skilled craftsmen.

THE ATSINA, who numbered about 3,000, are now at Ft. Belknap Res. in Montana. They are also called Gros Ventres (big bellies), although no stouter than their neighbors. Their name in Indian sign language was shown by circling the hands in front of the stomach, signifying "big belly."

THE ARAPAHO also numbered about 3,000. They had been corn-growers in Minnesota before coming to the High Plains. Although the Arapaho always fought the Shoshoni, they now live on the same reservation at Wind River, Wyoming.

THE ASSINIBOIN, who once numbered some 10,000, separated from their relatives, the Sioux, and later fought with them. In Chippewa language, *Assiniboin* means "one who cooks with stones." The Assiniboin are now at Ft. Belknap and Ft. Peck Res. in Montana.

SIOUX is a contraction of *Nadouessioux*. It means "enemies" in Chippewa, who fought the Sioux when they lived farther east. The Sioux, some 25,000 strong, invaded and spread west to the Rockies. They became known as Dakota, Nakota and Lakota, meaning "allies."

THE CHEYENNE were originally Minnesota farmers, but quickly adopted the ways of the Plains Indians. Numbering some 3,000, they seem to have covered more territory while hunting, warring and raiding than much larger tribes.

THE SUN DANCE was an ancient Plains ceremony to honor the buffalo and to insure good health and good hunting. The ceremony lasted for eight days. Most was taken up in secret rites, in fasting, prayers and other preparations. On the last day the public was invited to watch the participants pierce their flesh and endure pain to prove their courage and enlist the pity of the life-giving sun, the god of "good medicine."

CLOTHING, ORNAMENTS AND DECORATIONS blossomed out when trade goods, such as knives, cloth, beads, and guns, became available in the 1860's to the 1880's. Robes, parfleches, moccasins and buckskin shirts were decorated with dyed porcupine quills and glass beads. Men painted designs on tipis and shields. They carved beautiful pipe bowls of red catlinite and made long pipe stems of ash. Each tribe developed typical designs, and individual craftsmen became famous. See examples on pp. 32–33 and in local museums (pp. 148–150).

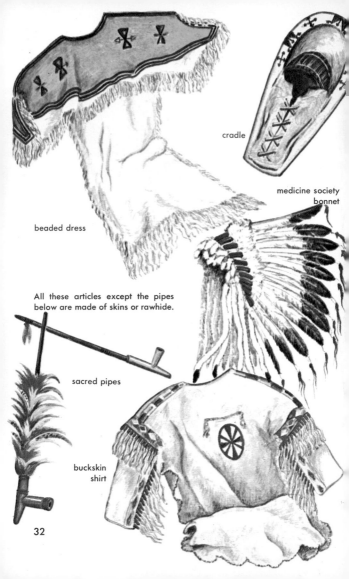

cradle

beaded dress

medicine society
bonnet

All these articles except the pipes
below are made of skins or rawhide.

sacred pipes

buckskin
shirt

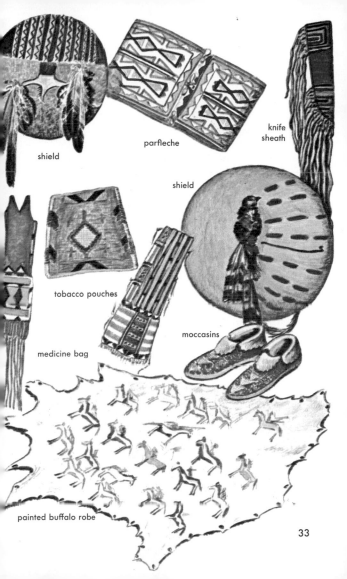

shield

parfleche

knife sheath

shield

tobacco pouches

medicine bag

moccasins

painted buffalo robe

33

EARLY EXPLORERS AND TRADERS The first white men to see the southern Rockies were Francisco Coronado and his men, who in 1540 marched north from Mexico in search of gold. None of these Spaniards entered the region covered by this book except for two parties that came into southern and western Colorado and into Utah in 1775-6 and these scarcely entered the Rockies.

During the 17th century a flourishing fur trade had developed throughout eastern North America to meet the European market for beaver, marten, muskrat, bear and buffalo. Beaver was in special demand for men's high felt hats, and the supply of these animals was rapidly exhausted. By the early 1700's trappers and traders, known as *voyageurs* and *coureurs de bois,* pushed westward along the rivers and through the Great Lakes. These French, English and Scotch adventurers traveled singly or in small parties. They lived with the Indians and some married Indian women. The knives and beads, guns and traps they brought were traded for furs, and Indians were encouraged to trap and hunt.

This 1728 map makes the first mention of the Rockies (far left)

Public Archives of Canada—from Trappers and Mountain Men. American Heritage Junior Library.

Vérendrye's two sons traveling westward towards the Rockies

One such *voyageur* from Quebec was Pierre Vérendrye who, with his four sons, had a trading post north of Lake Superior. Here as he traded, Vérendrye picked up stories of westward-flowing rivers and of "mountains that shine night and day." Later an Indian made a crude chart of the route to the west and put the Rocky Mountains on a map for the first time. Vérendrye pushed westward, building a series of trading posts. He moved on to the Mandan in 1738 and probably got as far west as the Black Hills in 1742–43. During the next 50 years it is estimated that some 5,000 *voyageurs* worked west of the Mississippi.

In 1763 a French trader, Pierre Laclede, and his 14-year-old stepson worked their way up the Mississippi to below the mouth of the Missouri. Here Laclede picked the site for a trading post, which he named St. Louis.

Trappers and Mountain Men. American Heritage Junior Library from Travels in the Interior of Nor
America. Maximilian, Prinz zu Wied-Neuwid Yale University Library

A contemporary artist pictures a Gros Ventre Indian attack on a keelboat at th
mouth of Montana's Bighorn River in 1833

THE UNITED STATES took over most of the Rockies a
part of the vast 827,000 square miles acquired as th
Louisiana Purchase from France in 1803. With $2,50
voted by Congress, and with President Jefferson's bless
ing, Meriwether Lewis and William Clark started to explor
the 15 million dollar purchase. They wintered in Manda
Indian villages in North Dakota and, with the help of
Shoshoni woman (p. 26), crossed the Rockies in 1805, re
turning the next year. About the same time, Zebulon Pik
headed west to discover the mountain that bears his name

The optimistic reports of Lewis and Clark sped Amer
can trappers on their trail. Within a year they were work
ing the upper Missouri and Platte rivers. One, John Colter
discovered the Yellowstone geysers. Soon competing com
panies were pushing their way into the Rockies. St. Loui
became the capital of the American fur trade by 1820. Fror
here keel boats went up the Missouri and its branches
carrying trade goods and bringing back furs.

Meanwhile, in Canada the Hudson's Bay Compan
merged with the North West Company in 1821 and com

36

bined their resources to push their fur trade into the Rockies where Flathead and Kutenai supplied the pelts. American companies were having their troubles with the Blackfoot and the Arikara. They hired agents, among others Mike Fink, Jedediah Smith and Jim Bridger, who recruited trappers and worked with them through the mountains from Montana to Colorado. Each year these mountain men met near the Green River in southern Wyoming to replenish supplies, to trade and to make merry. The last great rendezvous was held in 1837. Changing styles and overtrapping had brought the fur trade to a halt.

Another American, John Frémont, was a surveyor on a Missouri River expedition in 1838–41. He was joined by Kit Carson in exploring the Rockies. They moved west, and after a period in California, Frémont returned to survey Rocky Mountain passes for a transcontinental railroad. Information from this survey prepared the way for the cross-country rail link completed some ten years later.

Last great trade rendezvous along the Green River in Wyoming's Wind River Mountains in 1837

Salt Lake City as it appeared in 1867

MINING AND SETTLEMENT went hand in hand as the Rockies were opened up by traders and settlers.

At the time of the Louisiana Purchase, the territory the U.S. acquired had an estimated population of 50,000 to 80,000, mainly French. It also included a few descendants of the Spanish settlers who had come in 1763. Early settlements were trading centers, such as New Orleans and St. Louis.

Gold lured Americans westward in 1849. By 1880 over 200,000 had crossed the Mississippi River. Of these, 100,000 entered Colorado in the 1859 gold rush. Settlements rose with each new mining field, but many became ghost towns as the ore gave out. Mining in the Rockies was not as easy as it was in California. Not until 1890, when Guggenheim installed heavy machinery, did large-scale operations begin. Soon Colorado became the leader in the production of gold and silver (Cripple Creek) and also produced copper, lead and zinc, tin, molybdenum and uranium. Colorado has already produced a total of over six billion dollars in metals and other minerals.

Utah was settled in 1847 by Mormons fleeing from persecution. Miners, headed for the California gold fields, trekked through Salt Lake City. Many stayed on to farm and raise cattle. Some also found gold in Utah; later, copper, silver, petroleum and coal were discovered. Utah's uranium deposits represent 35% of the nation's total.

In Montana, gold was found in the early 1860's in the Miso River, in Alder Gulch, Virginia City, around Bannock, and in Last Chance Gulch. Helena became the capital. Today Montana still mines copper, silver, lead, zinc, aluminum, tungsten, uranium, petroleum and coal.

Idaho gold was found near Orofine in 1860; silver, in the Coeur d'Alene area in 1884. The gold rush brought settlers. Idaho became a territory in 1863 and a state in 1890. Idaho still mines copper, antimony, magnetite, zinc and phosphates.

Wyoming, too, has great mineral resources—coal, petroleum, bentonite, iron, copper, uranium, and phosphate. The first two are still of importance. But the first settlers in Wyoming came from farmlands and they turned mainly to raising sheep and cattle and to dairying

Helena, in the newly organized Montana Territory, from an 1865 print

Southern Pacific Railroad—from *Railroads in the Days of Steam*. American Heritage Junior Library

The joining of the rails in 1869 at Promontory, Utah, completed the first transcontinental railroad

RAILROADS AND SETTLEMENT   A network of railroads to unite the continent and encourage western settlement was proposed to Congress before the Civil War by Asa Whitney, a New York merchant. However, the costs were high and problems unprecedented. In 1864, the Northern Pacific Company was authorized by Congress to construct a railway from Lake Superior to Puget Sound, by a northern route. The Union Pacific Railroad Company was authorized to build a railroad from Omaha, Nebraska, through Wyoming, Utah and Nevada to California, joining the Central Pacific heading east from San Francisco.

Congress donated to each project a 400-foot right-of-way, all the stone, timber and earth needed, plus land grants of 12,800 acres for every mile of track constructed.

In addition the companies were given a 30-year loan, based on estimated costs per mile. Chinese and Irish laborers were imported. Machinery was brought around Cape Horn and overland. Bridges were built and tunnels bored. Herds of buffalo were slaughtered to feed the work crews.

In triumph over great hardships, the Union Pacific met the Central Pacific in 1869, 53 miles out of Ogden, Utah. By this time, the Chicago and Northwestern had reached Omaha and the Kansas Pacific had penetrated as far west as Denver, to join the Union Pacific at Cheyenne at

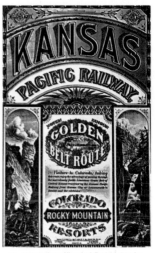

The Kansas State Historical Society, Topeka—from *Railroads in the Days of Steam*. American Heritage Junior Library

By the 1870's railroads were advertising for both settlers and visitors

later date. Now western farmers, cattlemen and miners had outlets for their products—both eastward and westward.

The railroads, struck by the 1873 depression, sent agents to the East and to Europe to attract settlers and to sell their huge land holdings. They offered settlers cheap transportation and financial help. They succeeded in getting many people to buy land. The region's population grew from under 200,000 in 1870 to almost a million and a half in 1890. This, and the fencing of the open range, settled the West.

HISTORICAL TIMETABLE

1540–1	Coronado explores the southern Rockies in New Mexico
1743	The Vérendryes visit the Wyoming Rockies
1776	Escalante penetrates north of Utah Rockies
1793	Alexander MacKenzie winters in the Canadian Rockies
1803	Louisiana Purchase includes eastern slope of Rockies
1805–06	Lewis and Clark cross and recross northern Rockies
1806–07	Pike explores the southern Colorado Rockies
1807	John Colter discovers the Yellowstone basin
1808–09	American and Missouri fur companies established
1811	Astoria-Hunt Expedition crosses central Rockies
1820	Long Expedition to Colorado; first ascent of Pikes Peak
1824	Great Salt Lake discovered by Jim Bridger and Peter Ogden
1825	First annual fur rendezvous, on Wyoming's Green River
1830	Rocky Mountain Fur Company organized
1834	Fort Hall becomes first major U.S. fort in Idaho Rockies
1841	California Trail through South Pass opened
1842	Frémont's first expedition. Establishment of Oregon Trail
1846	Northwestern Rockies acquired from Great Britain by U.S.
1847	Mormon settlers reach Great Salt Lake; establish State of Deseret
1848	Southwestern Rockies acquired from Mexico
1858	Gold rush to Colorado Rockies begins
1860	Pony Express inaugurated across Rockies to San Francisco
1861	Gold discovered in Idaho's Snake River Valley. Cheyenne-Arapaho Indian wars commence in Colorado
1863	Montana gold rush
1867	Salt Lake Mormon Tabernacle completed. Western Sioux War
1867–69	U.S. Geological Surveys in West commence
1869	First transcontinental rail links meet at Promontory, Utah
1871	Province of British Columbia enters Confederation
1872	Yellowstone created as first national park
1874	Black Hills gold rush starts
1876	Battle of the Little Big Horn (Custer's Last Stand) Colorado admitted to the Union as 38th state
1883	Northern Idaho's gold rush starts
1887	End of the open cattle range
1889	Montana becomes the 41st state
1890	Idaho (43rd state) and Wyoming (44th state) admitted to Union
1891	Cripple Creek, Colorado, gold rush starts
1896	Utah becomes 45th state in Union
1910	Casper, Wyo., oil boom, leading later to Teapot Dome scandal
1938	Big Thompson project, diverting water to Eastern Slope, begins
1958	U.S. Air Force Academy opens on Colorado foothills
1959	Yellowstone earthquake

The Front Range includes upraised and tilted sediments

THE GEOLOGIC STORY

Evidences of normal geologic cycles go back over a billion years. Seas invaded the land; layers of sediments formed; the land rose, forming mountains; volcanoes erupted. And with slow insistence sun, wind, rain, rivers, and ice leveled the land again. Life slowly developed. Some 60 million years ago a great series of sharp uplifts folded, squeezed and elevated the rocks to form the Rockies and the Andes. Later there was regional uplift. Volcanic action and deep movements of molten rock brought veins of rich ores. Glaciers have cut valleys, sharpened peaks, and created magnificent scenery.

For more about the rocks of the Rockies, read:

Dyson, J. L., GEOLOGIC STORY OF GLACIER NAT. PARK, Glacier Nat. Hist. Assn., Bull. #3, 1949

Fenneman, N. M., PHYSIOGRAPHY OF WESTERN U.S., McGraw-Hill, N.Y., 1931

Ross and Rezak, ROCKS AND FOSSILS OF GLACIER NAT. PARK, Geo. Sur. Prof. Paper #294-K, Govt. Printing Ofc., Wash., D.C., 1959

Wegemann, C. H., A GUIDE TO THE GEOLOGY OF ROCKY MT. NAT. PARK, Govt. Printing Ofc., Wash., D.C., 1944

Geological Time Divisions	Beginning of Interval (million years)	Major Events of This Time	Characteristic Life of Period
Cenozoic Era		Climate cold. Mountain and continental glaciation. Later, glacial lakes in mountain bases. Scattered volcanic action in Yellowstone and other areas.	Men entered the area from Asia via Alaska and the Northwest. Climate cold. With retreat of ice, remnants of arctic life remain isolated on mountain tops.
Quaternary Period			
Recent	.015		
Pleistocene	1		
Tertiary Period		Uplift of Rocky Mts. in several stages. Widespread crustal disturbances and volcanic eruption. Many inland lakes, swamps and flood plains. Local sedimentary deposits. Climate mild.	Mammals become dominant animals and spread widely. Grasses and other flowering plants develop, favoring development of camels, horses, and other grazing animals.
Pliocene	13		
Miocene	25		
Oligocene	36		
Eocene	58		
Paleocene	63		
Mesozoic Era		Widespread deserts give way to lowlands which are invaded by the sea. Fluctuating sea coasts with swamps and small basins. Rich sedimentary deposits.	Dinosaurs and other reptiles dominate. Birds develop and mammals appear. Cycads, tree ferns, conifers abound. Ammonites (p. 59) reach climax.
Cretaceous	135		
Jurassic	181		
Triassic	230		
Paleozoic Era		Continual marine invasion and deposition of sediments with periods of emergence. Abundant marine life. Swamps and coal formation. Era ends in sharp uplift, subsidence, erosion, and much aridity.	Marine invertebrates and plants are common. First marine vertebrates develop. Mosses and ferns appear; also giant amphibians and first reptiles.
Permian	280		
Pennsylvanian	310		
Mississippian	345		
Devonian	405		
Silurian	425		
Ordovician	500		
Cambrian	600		
Precambrian		Rocks, badly altered and recrystallized, indicate long geologic cycles of uplift and erosion. Extensive volcanic and marine deposits. Era ends with simple fossils showing first marine life.	Indirect evidence of conditions favorable to life—sunshine, wind, rain, rivers—at least a billion years ago. First algae and other simple unicellular or colonial life.
Keeweenawan	800		
Huronian	1050		
Timaskaming	1200		
Laurentian	2000		
	to		
Keewatin	3000		

Where Seen in
Rocky Mountains

Craters of the Moon, Yellowstone, Glacier National Park, Tetons, Rocky Mt. National Park, Wind River Mountains.

Green River and Uinta Basins, Absaroka Mountains, Devil's Tower, Middle Park, Florissant, Cripple Creek, Rocky Mt. National Park, and Black Canyon of the Gunnison.

Black Canyon of the Gunnison, Colorado National Mon., Dinosaur Nat. Mon., Wyoming Range.

Tetons, Gros Ventre Mt., Little Rocky Mts., Little Belt Mts., Garden of the Gods, Big Horn Mts., Banff, Lake Louise, Wind River Mts., Laramie Range, Aspen, Dinosaur Nat. Mon., Wyoming Range, Wasatch Range.

Black Canyon of the Gunnison, Colorado Nat. Mon., Uinta Mts., Glacier Park, Tetons, Rocky Mt. Nat. Park, Pikes Peak, Royal Gorge.

MOUNTAIN BUILDING in the Rockies is a tremendous, complex process differing from place to place. Nowhere is it as simple as the pictures show. When the oldest rocks were formed, about 2 billion years ago, the area had probably already gone through cycles of mountain building and destruction. Thick layers of sediments formed in the local seas. Later molten granite flowed into these sediments and the region was uplifted. The sediments were altered as a range of ancient mountains formed (1). These were slowly worn down until the land was again nearly flat (2). Seas encroached and new sediments were depos-

1 Ancient mountains of granite and altered sediments formed more than 600 million years ago.

2 Mountains worn flat; seas encroach; more sediments are deposited. About 350–550 million years ago.

The Tetons are a classic example of mountain building in the Rockies

George Wolfson

...ted in the shallow basins. Then followed a long period of fluctuation. Often the land was submerged and marine sediments were deposited. Sometimes it was elevated to form local mountains (3) which were again worn down by rain and running water.

During the Age of Reptiles (Mesozoic Era) extensive shallow seas covered western North America. Where land was uplifted it was low and swampy. Coal formed, and dinosaurs wallowed in swamps (4). Later the climate changed and became drier. Dinosaurs became extinct. A period of mountain building began all through the West.

3 Uplift creates local mountain ranges which are soon worn down. About 320 million years ago.

4 Seas cover wide area; local uplift with swamps, coal and lowland sediments. 100–200 million years ago.

5 Great uplift, folding and faulting mark beginning of present Rockies. About 60 million years ago.

6 Erosion, further uplift, and many volcanoes mark further growth of Rockies. 20–50 million years ago.

The modern Rockies started with uplifts squeezing and folding the rocks (5). Folds overturned and split; cracks or faults permitted further movements. This took millions of years. Erosion cut away the mountains. Later there was regional uplift with widespread volcanic action (6). Erosion continued; rivers cut deeper gorges. Then, as the climate changed, glaciers gouged the mountains (7). Much of North America was covered with ice. As it melted, great inland lakes formed and eventually drained. Only remnants of glaciers are seen in the Rockies (8) but earthquakes, as in Yellowstone in 1959, remind us that mountain building is not yet at an end.

7 More erosion; glaciation on mountains and northern plains. Several ice advances, 20–50,000 years ago.

8 Ice melts; glaciers retreat until only remnants and debris remain. Climate warming to present day.

tongue of the Columbia Icefield, Mt. Athabaska, Jasper National Park, Alberta

GLACIERS form when summers are not warm enough to melt the winter's accumulation of snow. The last great period of glaciation began about a million years ago. Snow piled up and changed to ice, and as ice became a mile or more thick it began to "flow." Continental glaciers moved south over eastern and central North America, N. Europe and Asia. In the high Rockies, smaller valley glaciers formed on mountain slopes and moved downhill, carving and deepening valleys on the way. The ice picked up rock debris which it dropped to form moraines. Three major advances and retreats of the ice sheets have been detected in the Rockies. About 20,000 years ago slightly higher temperatures started the last retreat. As ice melted, glacial lakes were formed. Deep U-shaped valleys were exposed, as were moraines and the cup-shaped cirques that mark the origin of glaciers. Today small valley glaciers are still seen, and evidence of earlier glaciation is everywhere. About a dozen prominent glaciers can be seen in the Rockies.

VALLEY GLACIERS are rivers of ice, moving only a few feet a year. When ice piles up faster than it melts, it flows slowly downhill carrying rock debris with it. When ice melts faster than it accumulates, the glacier retreats. A typical valley glacier is shown on p. 49.

MORAINES are glacial trash piles of rock, sand and gravel (glacial till) dumped along the sides, bottom and end of a glacier as it melts. A retreating glacier may leave a series of terminal moraines which occasionally hold small lakes. Above is a moraine in the Columbia Icefield, Jasper N.P.

CIRQUES mark the heads of glaciers. Here snow collects and changes to ice. Freezing and thawing break up the rock walls, enlarging the cirque. When glaciers melt the cirque remains, often enclosing a tiny lake of icy-blue water. Iceberg Lake fills a cirque (below) in Glacier N.P.

U-SHAPED VALLEYS cut by glaciers contrast with V-shaped valleys of swift rivers. Valley walls may show glacial polishing and grooving, evidence of glacial erosion. Glacial valleys, burdened with till, may contain small streams. This glacial valley runs east from Grinnell Glacier in Glacier N.P.

Hot springs with sulfur deposits (left) and Castle Geyser (right), in Yellowstone National Park

VOLCANIC ACTION in the Rockies has gone on for 50 million years. Old volcanoes, lava flows and mountains of igneous rocks (p. 52) are direct evidence. Secondary effects are seen as rain water works down to depths where the rocks are still heated. This water may return to the surface through steam vents or fumaroles, in hot springs, mud volcanoes and geysers. All these can be seen in Yellowstone National Park. Hot springs occur widely from Colorado north into the Canadian Rockies.

Cliff Geyser along the banks of Iron Creek, a tributary of the Firehole River

granite

pegmatite

basalt

IGNEOUS ROCKS form far below the surface (intrusive), or on the surface (extrusive). Intrusive rocks cool slowly; their minerals develop as crystals. *Granite* is interlocking crystals of quartz, feldspar and mica or another dark mineral. *Pegmatite* is a coarse granite. *Gabbro* is intrusive rock rich in dark minerals. Most extrusive rocks are volcanic. *Basalt,* a dark lava, may be dense or full of gas bubbles (scoria). *Obsidian* or volcanic glass is lava which has cooled rapidly. Some lavas are richer in quartz and feldspar. *Rhyolite* is chemically like granite. *Pumice* is a light, frothy rhyolite. Igneous rocks grade into one another so recognition may be difficult.

scoria

obsidian

pumice

52

SEDIMENTARY ROCKS form from fragments of older rock worn down by water, wind or ice, or by chemical action. These, the most common rocks in the Rockies, form in layers—the younger ones above the older. *Conglomerate* is pebbles or larger fragments cemented together; *Breccia* is a conglomerate of angular fragments. *Sandstone* is a rock of sand grains cemented by silica, lime or iron oxide. *Arkose,* a sandstone with grains of feldspar, typical of rapid erosion, is common in the Rockies. *Mudstone* and *shale* are hardened muds and clays. Shale splits into thin layers. *Limestone* comes from shells or coral, or is chemically deposited in the sea. *Gypsum* is deposited as landlocked seas evaporate slowly.

conglomerate

sandstone

arkose

mudstone

limestone

gypsum (alabaster)

METAMORPHIC ROCKS are rocks of any kind which have been altered in a major way by heat, pressure, or chemical action. Such alteration may take place during mountain building. The process may be simple, as when sandstones are compressed and hardened into *quartzite,* or when limestones become *marble*. Both of these rocks occur in the Rockies. Shales and mudstones become *slate,* and, if the process continues, *phyllite* forms with fine specks of mica. Further metamorphism produces *schist,* in which the mica is much more prominent. Sometimes metamorphism so alters rock that the original material cannot be recognized. *Gneiss* is a coarse-textured, partly recrystallized rock of various origins. Highly metamorphosed rocks may be similar to granite.

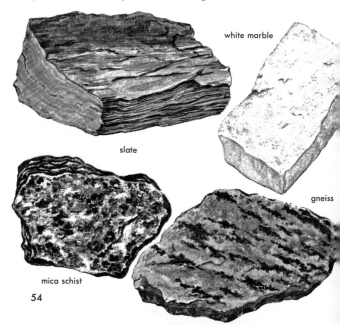

white marble

slate

gneiss

mica schist

ROCKY MOUNTAIN MINERAL AND ORE DEPOSITS

Sb	Antimony
Cu	Copper
Au	Gold
Fe	Iron
Pb	Lead
Mn	Manganese
Hg	Mercury
Mo	Molybdenum
Ag	Silver
Ta	Tantalum
Ti	Titanium
W	Tungsten
U	Uranium
Zn	Zinc

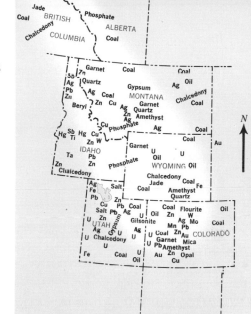

MINERAL DEPOSITS made the Rocky Mountains famous. Explorers were enticed by them. Indians were antagonized, prospectors rewarded, industries established, and settlements begun because of them. Gold and silver were the original attractions though these are no longer of prime importance. The region has rich deposits of copper, uranium and molybdenum, and commercial deposits of lead, zinc, tungsten, and iron. Coal deposits and natural gas are adequate; oil reserves (including oil shale) are plentiful. Non-metallic deposits include marble and other building stones, clays, feldspar, phosphates, fluorite, mica, and gypsum. A rich variety of gem and ornamental stones attracts amateur collectors.

ORES are deposits from which some product such as metals can be profitably extracted. Some yield a single metal; more often an ore complex yields several.

GOLD and SILVER are mainly invisible. Small but important amounts are found today. Only in the early days, when gold was panned in streams, did miners find visible gold. Even then, nuggets were rare.

CHALCOCITE, a dark, heavy ore of copper and sulfur, occurs widely with rich deposits near Butte, Montana.

MALACHITE and AZURITE, two copper ores, occur together. Formed by action of air and water on chalcocite.

GALENA is the major ore of lead, a compound of lead and sulfur often containing silver. A heavy silvery ore; often has cubic cleavage.

SPHALERITE or zinc blende is the zinc ore, a compound of zinc and sulfur. Its color varies from yellow to brown; often resinous.

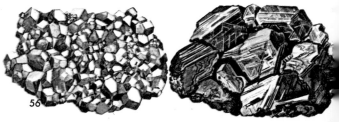

Usually the metal is in chemical combination and must be refined. Ores are generally associated with igneous rocks. They occur in veins or pockets.

CARNOTITE is a complex ore of uranium and vanadium. Usually found as yellow streaks or grains in sedimentary rocks.

MOLYBDENITE, a compound of molybdenum and sulfur, is a soft, metallic, flaky ore of the metal used in tool-steel alloys.

PYRITE, or fool's gold, is a bright shiny compound of iron and sulfur. Not an ore of iron, it is often associated with other ores.

GYPSUM, calcium fluoride, purple or green, occurs in veins. Mined commercially in Colo., it is used as a flux in steel making.

FELDSPARS are a group of silicate minerals found in most igneous rocks. Rich Colo. deposits are mined for ceramic flux and pottery glazes.

FLUORITE, formed by evaporation of ancient seas, is used in making plaster and cement. One form, alabaster, is carved and sold as curios.

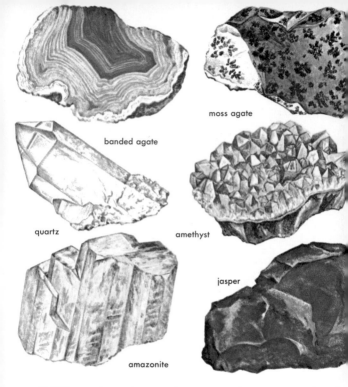

banded agate

moss agate

quartz

amethyst

jasper

amazonite

GEMS, semi-precious and ornamental stones, are found. Some, like topaz, corundum and beryl, occur in igneous veins or in pegmatite intrusions. Amazonite, a green feldspar from Pikes Peak, is an interesting local gem. Most common and best known are quartz gems. Crystalline quartz includes rock crystal, smoky quartz, citrine and amethyst. Noncrystalline quartz includes chalcedony, jasper, carnelians and several kinds of agates. Moss agate has inclusions of dendrites—a manganese mineral.

FOSSILS unequaled elsewhere in the world have been found in the Rockies and adjacent Plains. Cambrian shales of the Canadian Rockies have yielded remarkable invertebrate fossils. In the Mesozoic deposits of Colorado and Wyoming are bones of many giant dinosaurs. The basic research on these animals was done from fossils of this region. Fossils of early horses, pigs, camels and elephants have been dug up also. See reconstructed skeletons and restorations in museums (p. 148). Make inquiries about small-scale collecting in local fossil beds (p. 152).

ASTRASPIS, a primitive, jawless fish of Ordovician age (p. 44) from Canon City, Colo., is one of the oldest known fossil vertebrates.

AMMONITES, a large group of shell-fish with chambered shells, became extinct in the Cretaceous. Some were complex; 2–3 ft. in diameter.

INOCERAMUS, relative of the oysters, was an abundant animal in shallow seas when dinosaurs were at their height. Length 1–10 in.

OREODONTS were short-legged, pig-like, hoofed mammals of the Oligocene. Teeth and bones are common fossils in E. Colo., and Wyo.

DINOSAURS are a famed group of extinct reptiles which reached their peak during the Mesozoic Era. Some were as small as chickens, others the largest land animals known. These largest dinosaurs were swamp-dwelling plant eaters. Relatives of the dinosaurs included flying reptiles, marine lizards and crocodile-like reptiles.

BRONTOSAURUS, 70 ft. long, lived in marshes of Wyo. and Utah in Jurassic. Ate water plants. Estimated weight 35 tons.

STEGOSAURUS, a heavily armored, small-brained, plant-eating dinosaur about 20 ft. long. Fossils from the Jurassic of Wyoming and Utah.

DIPLODOCUS, longer but lighter, needed about 700 lbs. of plant food daily. Length, 85 ft.; height, 16 ft. Common at Dinosaur Nat. Mon.

TYRANNOSAURUS, largest flesh-eater, stood 20 ft. high. Length, 40 ft. Great jaws with many sharp teeth. Cretaceous; Montana.

ALPINE PHLOX (2–4 in.) forms a flat cushion amid alpine rocks. Is covered with pale blue or white five-petaled flowers in midsummer.

SKY PILOT (2–4 in.) blooms all summer with sky-blue, funnel-shaped flowers. Leaves, with skunky odor, are long, narrow; with oval leaflets.

ROCKY MOUNTAIN PLANTS

The formidable mountain backbone of North America is a varied region, ranging from the dry prairies to the east, up the mountains, with their lush meadows and forests, to the frigid peaks, then down to the even more arid intermountain region to the west. In these varied environments grow between 6,000 and 7,000 species of wild plants. Omitting the plains and the arid plateaus reduces the number to about 4,500 mountain species—ample proof that this area is rich in plant life.

Local conditions of elevation, slope, wind, rainfall, and soil affect plant environments. The pattern of plant communities is complex. For more information, read:

Craighead, Craighead, and Davis, FIELD GUIDE TO ROCKY MOUNTAIN WILD-FLOWERS, Houghton Mifflin Co., Boston, 1963. 209 full-color photos.

Nelson, R. A., PLANTS OF ROCKY MT. NATIONAL PARK, Washington, D.C., Government Printing Office, 1953. Excellent guide to central Rockies.

Standley, P. C., PLANTS OF GLACIER NATIONAL PARK, Washington, D.C., Government Printing Office, 1926. Similar to Nelson with emphasis on northern Rockies.

Weber, William A., HANDBOOK OF PLANTS OF THE COLORADO FRONT RANGE, University of Colorado Press, 1961. Keys and habitat notes on region from Colorado Springs to Wyoming line.

MOSS CAMPION (½–3 in.), commo
in the high Rockies, forms fla
"mossy" cushions. Small, pink flow
ers with notched petals bloom in Jul
and August.

ALPINE SUNFLOWER (4–6 in.) has
large, bright yellow flowers and stems
with deeply divided, hairy leaves. The
flower head turns with the sun.

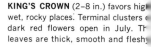

KING'S CROWN (2–8 in.) favors hig
wet, rocky places. Terminal clusters
dark red flowers open in July. Th
leaves are thick, smooth and fleshy

ALPINE AVENS (2–10 in.) is the com
monest flower above timberline. I
yellow, five-petaled flowers bloom i
midsummer. Deeply divided leaves a
red in autumn.

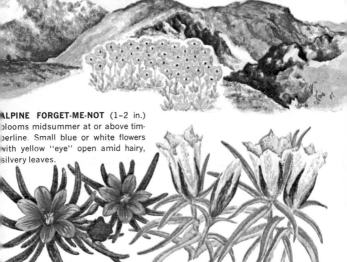

ALPINE FORGET-ME-NOT (1–2 in.) blooms midsummer at or above timberline. Small blue or white flowers with yellow "eye" open amid hairy, silvery leaves.

PYGMY BITTERROOT (1–3 in.), a small "cousin" of Montana's state flower, has narrow fleshy leaves in a cluster at ground level, and small pink or white flowers.

ARCTIC GENTIAN (3–6 in.) is common at and above timberline; blooms late (Aug. and Sept.). Flowers are greenish-streaked and spotted with purple. Leaves opposite.

AVALANCHE LILY (8–12 in.), with large, yellow flowers with six recurved petals, blooms on alpine slopes right after the receding snow line.

63

FLOWERS OF THE SUBALPINE HEIGHTS

WHITE MARSH MARIGOLD (3–8 in.) thrives in moist subalpine areas. The oval leaves are smooth and shiny. Fruits are a cluster of narrow pods.

PYROLA (6–12 in.) bears nodding, five-petaled, pink flowers on stem from a rosette of shiny, evergreen leaves. Common in moist coniferous woods. Several similar species.

PURPLE FRINGE (2–12 in.) grows in small clumps on open, dry hillsides. Flowers from June to Aug. Silky hairs on deeply divided leaves make plant silvery.

TWINFLOWER (3–6 in.) carries its paired, pink, nodding blossoms on upright stalks. The creeping plant with opposite leaves covers the ground in cool, shady woods.

PARRY PRIMROSE (6–24 in.) grows along mountain streamsides. Its large, five-petaled, pink-purple flowers are skunk-scented. It blooms in July and August.

SUBALPINE DAISY (1–2 ft.) is the common meadow daisy flowering in July and Aug. Note its narrow, pink ray-flowers, around a yellow disc. Leaves are deeply cut.

RED ELEPHANT (1–2 ft.) prefers marshy ground. Reddish-purple flowers, with a comical resemblance to elephants' heads, bloom in a terminal spike.

TALL CHIMING BELLS (1–2 ft.), with pink buds and nodding blue blossoms, are found along subalpine brooks. Blooms June to Aug. Several similar species.

COLORADO COLUMBINE (1–2 ft.), state flower of Colorado, prefers aspen groves and high meadows. Look for large, blue-and-white, spurred blossoms on slender stalks.

MONUMENT PLANT (1–4 ft.) is a stout plant of open pine woods and clearings. Upper half of its leafy stem is thickly covered with greenish-white flowers.

BEARGRASS (2–5 ft.) grows on hillsides to and above timberline in Montana and Idaho. Tiny flowers bloom upward gradually from base of terminal cluster.

GLOBEFLOWER (1–2 ft.) prefers high, subalpine meadows. Cream to white flowers produce a group of small pods. Leaves are alternate, divided into 5–7 smooth "fingers."

WESTERN GOLDEN RAGWORT (1–3. ft.), one of many similar composites. Found along roadsides up to timberline. This species is bushy with many flowers.

YELLOW MONKEYFLOWER (6–24 in.) is abundant on brook sides. Flowers have a swollen "palate" which closes the throat and causes a facial resemblance.

ROSY PAINTBRUSH (6–15 in.) has pink to purple flower bracts. Hybridization with white- and yellow-flowered species produces a great variety of colors.

SUBALPINE LARKSPUR (2–4 ft.) grows in dense clumps in wet meadows close to timberline. Terminal spikes of deep blue (rarely, pink) spurred flowers.

FIREWEED (2–5 ft.) grows widely in the open, particularly on burned-over forests; hence its name. Winds carry the downy seeds for great distances. A great honey plant.

MONKSHOOD or Aconite (to 6 ft.) has cowl-shaped, deep blue (rarely, white) flowers. Grows in subalpine meadows and aspen groves. Poisonous to grazing stock.

67

FLOWERS OF THE FOOTHILLS AND MOUNTAIN VALLEYS

SCARLET GILIA, or Sky-rocket (1–2 ft.), is a handsome perennial with trumpet-shaped, red to cream flowers in a loose cluster. Abundant in canyons and sagebrush.

SULPHUR FLOWER (5–15 in.), abundant in dry subalpine foothills, has clusters of yellow flowers and whorled leaves rising from a rosette.

STRAWBERRY BLITE (6–18 in.) is named for its clusters of tiny red fruits, resembling strawberries, along the stem. Its leaves are roughly triangular.

BLUE FLAX (1–2 ft.) bears delicate blue flowers on slender stalks. Flowers are common on hillsides but close before noon and are therefore often missed.

GOLDEN PEA (6–18 in.) blankets valley floors with bright-yellow flowers in June and July. Leaves have three leaflets, like clover.

GAILLARDIA (1–2 ft.) blooms all summer in foothills, woods, and meadows. Its yellow flower heads have reddish centers. Also called "Fire-wheels."

WESTERN WALLFLOWER (1–2 ft.), common on open pine slopes, has four-petaled, yellow-to-orange and brown flowers. Alpine types may be pure yellow or violet.

BALSAM ROOT (8–18 in.) grows from thick, edible, turpentine-scented taproot. Leaves are silky and white on both sides. Common on hillsides; blooms early spring.

RABBIT BRUSH (8–24 in.), a dense shrub (source of rubber) with narrow leaves and woolly stems in sagebrush zone. Small yellow heads in late summer.

SHOOTINGSTARS (6–10 in.) are woodland and wet-meadow plants. The flowers, with five inverted petals, grow in drooping clusters. Leaves at base of tall, naked flower stalk.

MANY-FLOWERED EVENINGSTAR (6–12 in.) opens its showy yellow flowers in late afternoon. Has salmon-colored buds and thick, deeply notched leaves.

MINER'S CANDLE (8–18 in.) has clusters of small white flowers along its thick, erect stem. Leaves hairy, almost prickly. Blooms June and July.

MOUNTAIN LUPINE (1–2 ft.) is also called Silvery Lupine because of its white hairy foliage. Blue to purple spikes of flowers bloom in early summer.

ROCKY MOUNTAIN LOCOWEED (10–18 in.) bears white or lavender flowers in elongated clusters from spring through summer. It is sometimes poisonous to cattle.

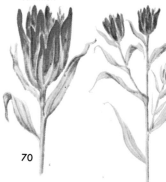

INDIAN PAINTBRUSH (1–3 ft.) has brilliant red bracts surrounding the blossoms. Partially parasitic, it often grows attached to roots of sagebrush and other plants.

MOUNTAIN HAREBELL (6–24 in.) blooms late. Its drooping blue bells, several to each slender stem, are seen among rocks well into fall, often above timberline.

CALYPSO (3–6 in.), or Fairy Slipper, is a lovely orchid blooming in early summer in moist woods. Delicate, slipper-like blossom nods above a single leaf.

HEARTLEAF ARNICA (8–24 in.) is common in evergreen woods. Large, yellow flowers bloom all summer. Note the pairs of large heart-shaped leaves.

MARIPOSA LILY (6–18 in.) bears tulip-like flowers, white or purplish, on slender stems. Blooms in open meadows and margins of woods in early summer.

WESTERN CLEMATIS is a vine common in the foothills. Note clusters of white flowers, conspicuous feathery fruits, and leaves of 5–7 leaflets.

71

SNOW-ON-THE-MOUNTAIN (1–3 ft.) is related to Poinsettia. Note the white margins of the upper leaves. Its milky sap is poisonous and may irritate skin.

TALL PENSTEMON (1–3 ft.) bears large, purplish flowers in one-sided spikes. It blooms in midsummer, sometimes turning whole fields blue.

SCARLET GLOBEMALLOW (4–10 in.) forms clumps on disturbed soil, especially along roadsides. Flowers resemble small hollyhocks or hibiscus.

ROCKY MOUNTAIN FRINGED GENTIAN (12–16 in.) is found in wet meadows or swamps. Its striking, deep-blue flowers have ragged lobes.

ROCKY MOUNTAIN BEE PLANT forms dense stands 4–8 feet high along roadsides and in dry places. Its flowers' rich nectar attracts bees and other insects.

72

CONIFERS OF UPPER FOREST AND TIMBERLINE

LPINE LARCH, or Tamarack (to 60 .), has clusters of many deciduous eedles growing from short shoots. ones, 2 in. long, have pointed bracts etween scales. Often a stunted tim- erline tree. New twigs are covered ith white wool. Foliage blue-green.

NGELMANN SPRUCE (60–120 ft.) orms pure stands but is also found ith Lodgepole Pine and Subalpine r. Ranges from 3,000 ft. in north to 2,000 in south. Compact and hand- ome, and of great commercial value. oung trees may have a silvery tinge.

SUBALPINE FIR grows 50–100 ft. but may be a prostrate shrub at timber- line. Needles are flat, deep blue-green, blunt and upcurved. Cones are dark and, as with all firs, erect. Cone scales fall separately, leaving the "candle" standing on the tree.

LIMBER PINE (25–60 ft.), named for flexible young branches; grows in rocky, exposed places. Needles, 3 in., are crowded in bundles of 5 at ends of twigs. Cone scales are thickened but not spine-tipped. Whiteheart Pine replaces it in northern Rockies.

73

BROAD-LEAVED TREES AND SHRUBS OF THE

WILLOWS of many species, nearly all shrubs, grow in profusion along streams and on slopes near timberline. Illustrated is Creeping Willow, a shrub that stands only 2 in. high and grows above timberline in Montana and Wyoming. All willows have catkins or "pussies."

MOUNTAIN DRYAS is a low, creeping shrub with small, toothed leaves, woolly beneath, and whitish, eight-petaled flowers. Forms dark green mats above timberline. A typical alpine plant found in high mountains of North America, Asia and Europe.

WATER BIRCH (10–25 ft.) is a spreading shrub or small tree with reddish-brown, non-peeling bark and twigs covered with resinous lumps. It is always found close to streams. Leaves turn a beautiful yellow in autumn. Bog Birch is a timberline shrub.

TWINBERRIES (3–6 ft.) are true honeysuckles. Small, yellow, tubular flowers are borne in pairs on a slender stem. Bracts at their base later turn red and enclose two purplish-black berries. Deer and elk browse on them in winter.

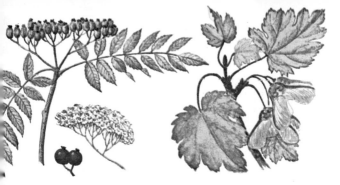

PPER FORESTS AND TIMBERLINE

MOUNTAIN ASH (3–12 ft.) is a shrub, sometimes a small tree. Large clusters of white flowers and brilliant orange-red berries in fall. Found mainly in subalpine zone in moist sites; planted ornamentally at lower ranges. Serviceberry is in same (Rose) family.

ROCKY MOUNTAIN MAPLE is sometimes a tree 25 feet high but more often a shrub of wide altitude range. The leaf has several forms, from typical maple shape to three completely separate lobes. The leaves turn pale yellow in autumn.

CINQUEFOILS (½–3 ft.) occur in many species. Their bright yellow, buttercup-like flowers with five-notched petals bloom from early spring to late summer from foothills to above timberline. Illustrated is Shrubby Cinquefoil, only woody species of the Rockies.

DWARF MOUNTAIN LAUREL (4–12 in.), an evergreen shrub found along streams; has clusters of pink, parasol-like flowers. Leaves are opposite, green above, white below, and edges often rolled under. Stamens "trigger" pollen spray when disturbed.

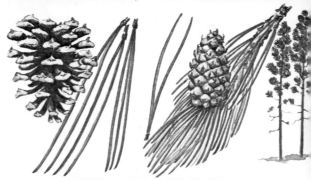

CONIFERS OF THE LOWER MOUNTAINS

WESTERN YELLOW PINE, or Ponderosa (80–180 ft.), forms open forests. Trunk rises straight and is sometimes branchless most of its length. Needles are in bunches of 2–3; bark of older trees breaks into large irregular plates. Very important as a lumber tree.

LODGEPOLE PINE (60–100 ft.) grows in dense stands after forest fires. Indians used slender poles for tipis; lumber has many uses. Needles, about 2 in. long, are in bunches of 2–3; cones are small; remain on tree many years; open after fires.

WESTERN WHITE PINE (90–120 ft.) is a tall, slender conifer with crown of short, drooping branches bearing needles in bundles of 5; has elongated cones. Sometimes one branch extends 10–15 ft. farther out than others. Wood very important commercially.

BRISTLECONE PINE (30–40 ft.) holds longevity record, 4,600 years, for trees. Bark is whitish when young; red-brown later. Cones are small; curved needles in bunches of 5, have dots of white resin. Trunk often twisted; a shrub at high elevations.

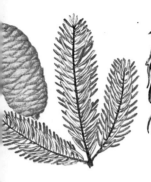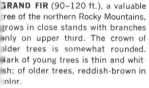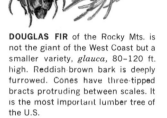

GRAND FIR (90–120 ft.), a valuable tree of the northern Rocky Mountains, grows in close stands with branches only on upper third. The crown of older trees is somewhat rounded. Bark of young trees is thin and whitish; of older trees, reddish-brown in color.

DOUGLAS FIR of the Rocky Mts. is not the giant of the West Coast but a smaller variety, *glauca,* 80–120 ft. high. Reddish-brown bark is deeply furrowed. Cones have three-tipped bracts protruding between scales. It is the most important lumber tree of the U.S.

DWARF JUNIPER, most widely distributed conifer of N. Hemisphere, is a sprawling shrub found both on barren slopes and in thick timber. The bark is reddish and scaly; needles are short, white above. The short, scale-leaves are awl-shaped.

ROCKY MOUNTAIN JUNIPER, about 15 ft., is a small bushy tree, reduced to a low shrub on exposed sites. Found on dry mountain slopes and canyon bottoms. Trunk often branched; bark, thin and stringy. Twigs are covered with tiny scale-like leaves.

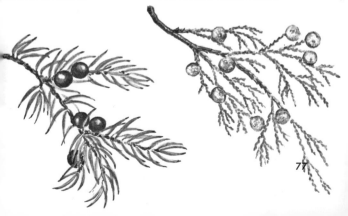

Blue Spruce

BLUE SPRUCE (80–100 ft.), the state tree of Colo., favors canyon stream-sides; is widely used as an ornamental. Needles are short, very sharp-tipped, often very white. Bark is dark, rusty, thin and scaly, becoming thick and furrowed on older trunks.

WESTERN LARCH (100–180 ft.) is typically a tall, narrow tree, even when growing in open. Branches short and tough; cones small, thickly scattered. Foliage pale green, becoming yellow in early fall and dropping from tree. Not found in the southern Rockies.

WESTERN HEMLOCK (120–160 ft.) has reddish, flaky bark, small cones. The flat, short, glossy needles of irregular length give a lacy appearance to the twigs. Trunk tapers to slender, weak point, typically drooping. Similar to hemlock found in East.

WHITE CEDAR (120–200 ft.), an impressive, often tall tree, is important for its durable, aromatic, but weak lumber. Limbs point upward at acute angles; branchlets carry flat, fern-like sprays. Typically a Pacific Coast tree. Found in Glacier Nat. Park.

BROAD-LEAVED TREES OF MOUNTAIN VALLEYS AND FOOTHILLS

COTTONWOODS are conspicuous in autumn when their foliage turns brilliant orange-yellow. **Narrowleaf Cottonwood** (35–50 ft.), illustrated here, has narrow leaves resembling those of willows. Common in Rocky Mountain and Yellowstone National Parks.

THINLEAF ALDER (6–20 ft.) forms dense thickets in saturated soil, and is useful in retarding erosion on banks and headwaters of streams. Easily recognized by the two types of catkins, the seed-bearing ones resembling small pine cones.

BALSAM POPLAR (50–80 ft.) is found commonly in moist bottomlands in mixed groves with alder, birch and spruce. Widely distributed in northern U.S. and Canada. Easily confused in the West with Black Cottonwood. Buds are sticky and aromatic.

GAMBEL OAK (10–15 ft.), a shrub or small tree of dry hillsides and canyon walls. It is the only abundant deciduous oak in Rockies. Bark is gray and rough; leaves are typically oak-shaped, dark green above, pale below. A widespread and variable species.

PAPER BIRCH (30–70 ft.) Indians made canoes from its creamy white bark. The surface peels off paper-thin. Often found near streams and lakes in mixed stands with aspen, poplar and tamarack. A tree of the northern and Canadian Rockies.

QUAKING ASPEN (40–60 ft.) is widespread in the Rockies. It quickly covers new burns and provides shelter under which conifers develop. Leaves with flattened petioles tremble in the slightest breeze. A favorite beaver food. Related to cottonwoods (p. 79).

PEACHLEAF WILLOW (50–70 ft.) is the only "tree" willow native to the Rockies and is easily identified by its tapered leaves, drooping branches and crooked trunk or trunks. Twigs are slender, pliable; bark of trunk is furrowed and sometimes reddish.

BLACK HAWTHORN (6–25 ft.), a shrub or small tree, often forms dense thickets on mountainsides or bottom lands. Branches with stout, purplish-red thorns. Showy, five-petaled white flowers. It has black fruits, like tiny apples, hanging in clusters.

SHRUBS OF MOUNTAIN VALLEYS AND FOOTHILLS

NINEBARK (5–10 ft.) is a spreading shrub with paper-like bark that peels off in layers. It bears white flowers in early summer and produces 2–3 inch flat seed pods. The toothed, hairy leaves have 3 to 5 lobes. Sometimes used in cultivation.

SQUAWBUSH, or Skunkbush (2–7 ft.), is a close relative of poison ivy but is harmless, though ill-smelling. Leaves with 3 leaflets and tiny yellow-green flowers appear early in spring. Indians make baskets from slender shoots and a drink from sticky red berries.

CHOKECHERRY (6–30 ft.) forms dense thickets that sprout from root suckers and make a brilliant show of red foliage in fall. Pea sized, black or dark red cherries are profuse and are a staple food of bears. Also used to make jelly by mountain housewives.

BUFFALO BERRY (2–8 ft.) prefers moist, shaded slopes. Branches are brown and scaly; leaves are dark green above and covered on underside with star-like scales. A relative, Russian-olive, is a favorite dryland shade tree.

SQUAW or **WAX CURRANT** (1–4 ft.), a shrub of dry slopes and ridges, has alternate palmate leaves, pink flowers, red fruit. Gooseberries (usually thorny) and other currants are also abundant.

MOUNTAIN LOVER (½–4 ft.), a low evergreen shrub of moist open woods. The leaves are leathery and slightly toothed, with very short stems; grow opposite on sprawling branches.

RED-OSIER DOGWOOD (4–8 ft.) bears flat-topped clusters of small white blossoms which mature into whitish fruits. Often forms thickets; dark red branches conspicuous in winter. Varieties with yellow bark are cultivated.

BITTERBRUSH, or Antelope Brush (2–8 ft.), is a browse plant of deer and antelope. A tough, widely branched shrub with pale yellow blossoms. Leaves are three-pronged, green above and white underneath.

82

SNOWBERRY (2–5 ft.), named for its large white berries, is eaten by deer and birds. The flowers are pink and hairy inside. Leaves are variable, thin and oval, and may be slightly hairy.

SERVICEBERRY (2–6 ft.) forms dense thickets. Its flowers, white with 5 long, narrow petals, bloom in late spring. Its purplish-black berries were an important food of Blackfoot Indians.

SAGEBRUSH, in many varieties, grows from 1–12 ft. in southern and central Rockies. Foliage silvery gray; three-pronged leaves are very aromatic. These common shrubs prefer deep, alkali-free soils.

THIMBLEBERRY (3–8 ft.) has a flattened raspberry-like fruit eaten by birds and other wildlife. Its delicate white flowers measure two inches across. This common shrub is not thorny.

REDBERRIED ELDER (1–3 ft.) A sprawling shrub with weak, pithy stems and opposite, compound leaves. It bears large clusters of small, white flowers. Has scarlet berries in fall.

OREGON HOLLYGRAPE (½–1 ft.) has holly-like leaves that turn deep red in fall. The flowers are yellow, in dense clusters. Berries are blue and make fine jelly. Prefers rocky gulches.

WHORTLEBERRIES are shrubs with small pink or white nodding flowers. All have toothed leaves. The dwarf form (Broom Huckleberry) has red berries; the berries of a taller species (1–3 ft.) are black.

BEARBERRY (½–1 ft.) is a prostrate evergreen shrub which often carpets the forest and pioneers on rocky slopes and new burns. Leaves are browsed by deer; red berries are a preferred food of grouse.

84

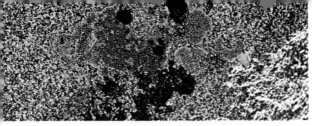

Lichens growing on a rock

Herbert S. Zim

NON-FLOWERING PLANTS range from minute bacteria to great conifers. Usually we think of the term as applying to ferns and their kin—mosses, liverworts, lichens, fungi and algae. All occur in the Rockies, and while most are neither large nor conspicuous, they are very common. About 25 ferns and a dozen fern allies can easily be found. With diligence the interested amateur can identify scores of mushrooms, lichens and mosses. Illustrated are just a few of the most commonly seen ferns, mosses and lichens of the Rockies.

BRITTLE FERN (½–1 ft.) takes its name from its thin, fragile stem. Grows from creeping black rootstock in very moist, shady areas. Very common in Rocky Mountain National Park; less so in Glacier.

WESTERN BRACKEN (1–5 ft.) is a stout, coarse fern with tough leathery fronds, often 6 ft. long. Some western Indians used young shoots as food. Grows in sandy or acid soils in all temperate regions.

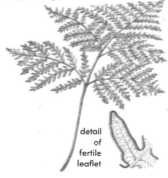

detail of fertile leaflet

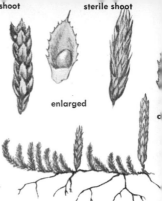

enlarged

ROCK BRAKE, or Parsley Fern (6–12 in.), has two kinds of fronds—leafy and spore-bearing. Grows on rocks and cliffs, usually in tight clumps. Found from the Rockies to the Pacific.

LICHENS are primitive plants composed of a food-producing alga and a supporting fungus. They pioneer in soil formation. Some are deer food; some sources of tannin and dyes.

SPIKE MOSS, or Little Club Moss, is slender branching moss-like plant related to ferns. Spores borne in axils of small leaves. Found on dry barren ground near rocks.

HAIRYCAP MOSS, a wiry-stemmed moss of dry, sunny soil or rocks, grows 3–5 in. high. The four-angled capsule sheds spores when ripe. Leaf margins fold back to the center.

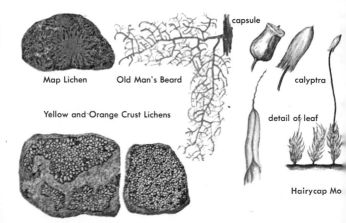

capsule

Map Lichen   Old Man's Beard

calyptra

Yellow and Orange Crust Lichens

detail of leaf

Hairycap Moss

HOARY MARMOT is a large (25–31 in.) alpine rodent restricted to northern Rockies. Gray with black-and-white face. Compare with more common Yellow-bellied Marmot, p. 91.

ANIMAL LIFE OF THE ROCKIES

A century ago wealthy European sportsmen came to the Rockies to hunt the famed grizzly and other bears, deer, elk, moose, mountain lions and mountain sheep. Such big game still roam the parks and mountains. Under a wise and strict conservation policy their numbers are increasing, and big game hunting is still important. However, the average visitor is more likely to get his thrill from the birds and smaller mammals than from an occasional glimpse of a large beast. Here are the most common species of the Rockies. Remember, all wildlife is protected in National Parks and in National Monuments. Try hunting with a camera. If you prefer a gun or fishing rod, check state and local laws and regulations.

For more information about mammals, read:

Burt & Grossenheider, A FIELD GUIDE TO THE MAMMALS, Houghton Mifflin, Boston, 1952

Palmer, Ralph S., THE MAMMAL GUIDE, Doubleday, N.Y., 1954

Rodeck, H. G., GUIDE TO THE MAMMALS OF COLORADO, Univ. of Colorado Museum, Boulder, Colo., 1952

Jim and Hoffmeister, MAMMALS, Golden Press, N.Y., 1955

MOUNTAIN SHEEP, or Bighorns (4–
5½ ft.), are elusive. Grayish-brown
with creamy-white rump and massive,
backward-curving horns, they prefer
grassy mountain areas. Females give
birth to one lamb born in spring.

MOUNTAIN GOAT (5½ ft.) looks lik
an all-white goat, but is more closel
related to antelope. Lives among al
pine cliffs. Color blends well wit
snow-covered rocks. Male and femal
look alike.

PIKA, or Cony (8 in.), lives in timberline rock slides. Pikas are gray-brown,
rabbit-like, with small, round ears and
no apparent tails. They gather, dry,
and store grass for winter food.

NORTHERN POCKET GOPHER (10 in.
a grayish-brown rodent of mt. mead
ows, lives underground and burrow
for fleshy roots. Piles of dirt mark th
tunnel entrances. Does not hibernate

88

MAMMALS OF FORESTS AND HIGH SLOPES

BLACK BEAR (300 lb.) is black or cinnamon with a brown face. Lacks shoulder hump of grizzly. Most common and widely distributed bear, it is seen near camps and roads. Eats almost everything.

MARTEN (25 in.), a forest carnivore, has long, slender body, short legs, brown, bushy tail and soft, dense, tur. Wt. 2-4 lb. Does not hibernate. Feeds on rodents, birds and eggs.

GRIZZLY BEAR, weighing up to 1,000 lb. and almost 7 ft. long, is the largest mountain carnivore. Its yellowish, white-tipped hairs give it a grizzled appearance. Feeds on game, fruits, and berries.

MINK (25 in.) hunts fish, frogs, crayfish, birds, and small mammals. An active carnivore similar to the weasel; always lives near water. Note its white chin patch. 4-10 young.

LONG-TAILED WEASEL (15–20 in., 3–8 oz.), is a widespread hunter of rodents and small birds; changes from brown to white in winter and is then called ermine. Has musky odor; 4–8 young born in spring.

RIVER OTTER (4–5 ft.), hunted for its beautiful thick fur, is an excellent web-footed swimmer. Eats fish, frogs, small mammals. Rich brown above, silvery below. Makes its den in burrows or thickets.

BOBCAT (30–50 in., 15–30 lb.). Alert and stealthy, the bobcat hunts by day as well as at night. It preys on small rodents and birds, rarely on larger animals. The bobcat prefers rocky thickets and dens in caves or hollow trees. Its color ranges from brown to gray, spotted with black.

RED FOX (35–40 in.) has three color phases—black, red, and cross. Usually red-dish-yellow with black "stockings" and white-tipped bushy tail. Lives in hollow logs and burrows; eats rodents, occasionally fruit.

**GOLDEN MANTLED GROUND SQUIR-
REL** (10 in.) is similar to Eastern
chipmunk but lacks head stripes. Has
coppery head, white body stripes bordered with black. A common camp
visitor in the Rockies.

RICHARDSON'S GROUND SQUIRREL
(11 in.) is smoky-gray with a light-
bordered tail. Often called Picket-Pin
from habit of sitting up straight. May
hibernate from 8 to 9 months in the
north or in dry areas.

YELLOW-BELLIED MARMOT (23 in.) is
yellowish, heavy-bodied rodent that
lives in burrows or under rocks. Feeds
on plants on rocky hillsides in the
southern Rockies.

MOUNTAIN LION, or Puma (80–200
lb., 6–8 ft.), is a large, long-tailed,
tawny cat that preys on deer and
other large mammals. Ranges widely
but is seldom seen. Two spotted young
are born each year.

91

BUSHY-TAILED WOOD RAT (15 in.) also called Pack or Trade Rat, steal small objects; may leave others in exchange. Builds large stick nests i rocky crevices, mine tunnels an under cabins.

PINE SQUIRREL, or Chickaree (13 in.) usually nests high in spruce or fir Yellowish-red in summer; grayer in winter. Feeds on seeds, nuts an fungi. It is noisy and an agile climber.

BEAVER (3 ft.) has fur so valuabl that it led to exploration of this region Builds houses and dams of mud an sticks. Swims with webbed hind feet Slaps water with flat tail as warning Feeds on bark and water plants.

MULE DEER (6 ft., 150–300 lb.) i habits open forests. It is reddis brown in summer, grayer in winte Has a mule-like tail and large ear Hunted by coyote, bear, puma an man. Female smaller; lacks antler

DEER MOUSE (7 in.) is a big-eared, white-bellied rodent found nearly everywhere. Nocturnal in habit, it feeds on anything edible; also stores seeds and fruits for winter. It is often seen around camps.

SNOWSHOE HARE (18 in., 2–4 lb.) is a short-eared, common mountain rabbit. Large "snowshoe" hind feet permit it to run over soft snow. Cottontails are also plentiful in the Rockies.

PORCUPINE (25–30 in., 10–28 lb.) is a short-legged, clumsy rodent covered with barbed quills which are loose but cannot be thrown. It is a slow, cautious climber, feeds on bark and twigs, especially of poplar.

ELK, or Wapiti (7–9 ft., 500–900 lb.), grazes on many plants. Spends winters in valleys, summer in mountains. Antlers are shed in March. Female is smaller; does not have antlers. One calf is born in the spring.

MAMMALS OF VALLEYS AND FOOTHILLS

STRIPED SKUNK (24 in., 4–8 lb.) lives in burrows, rocky crevices, or under logs and buildings. Eats insects, mice, fruit and carrion. Spotted Skunk of southern Rockies is smaller.

BADGER (25 in., 10–20 lb.) is heavy-bodied and short-legged. A powerful digger, it hunts rodents in their burrows; also eats birds, eggs, reptiles and insects. May mound dirt at burrow entrances.

WHITE-TAILED JACK RABBIT (24 in.) ranges from prairies to timberline. Prefers open country; relies on speed for protection. Leaps 15–20 ft. Is brownish in summer, whitish in winter.

13-LINED GROUND SQUIRREL (10 in.) eats seeds, plants, insects, grubs and worms. Shy and quick, it hibernates in winter. Has beaded, brownish stripes on sides and back.

WHITE-TAILED PRAIRIE DOG (13 in.) is a rodent of mountain grasslands; lives in "towns" or colonies. Stands guard on mounds, uttering a high-pitched bark when alarmed.

MUSKRAT (22 in.) lives in burrows in pond banks or in conical houses of matted vegetation. Eats aquatic plants. The long tail is flattened vertically. It is an important fur bearer.

TUFT-EARED SQUIRREL (20 in.) is a pine forest dweller. Its ears are tufted except in late summer. It varies in color; is often gray above and white below but may be all black.

LEAST CHIPMUNK (7 in.) is the smallest chipmunk in Rockies. When alarmed it runs with tail upright. Lives in burrows under stumps or rocks; stores seeds, nuts, and fruits for winter.

COYOTE (3½ ft.) is a smaller relative of the wolf; holds its tail down when running. It eats rodents and other small animals, grasshoppers and fruit. Its often-heard yapping is distinctive.

PRONGHORN (5 ft., 90–130 lb.), our fastest mammal, is a unique American species and is not an antelope. Tan, with white under and on rump. It eats shrubs and grass on open ranges; sheds horn covers yearly.

MOOSE (700–1300 lb.), the largest of the deer family, lives in swampy valleys and along streams. Eats aquatic plants, shrubs and bark. Males have large, broad, flattened antlers.

BISON, or Buffalo (12 ft.), once roamed the Plains in millions. Slaughtered for meat and hides, only rigid conservation preserved the species. Shoulder height is 6 ft.; weight up to 1 ton.

TRUMPETER SWAN (65 in.) breeds on a few Rocky Mountain lakes. It was once near extinction, but now has a population of about 1,500 birds.

WHITE PELICAN (55–70 in.) has black primaries and a yellow throat pouch. Soars gracefully; does not dive for food. Nests on inland lakes.

BIRDS OF THE ROCKIES

With a range of elevation exceeding 10,000 feet, there is a corresponding variation in bird population. Along the front ranges of the Rockies, eastern species are common. Here is part of the central flyway along which many water-fowl species migrate north from Mexico and Central America. Moving up the foothills through the forests and alpine meadows brings marked changes in bird life. The seasons produce more changes. In winter, alpine and northern species move southward and down the mountains. The local environment also exerts an influence. Some birds prefer lakes and streams; others, open woods; and a few species prefer the cold of mountain heights.

For more about birds of the Rockies, read:

Niedrach and Rockwell, BIRDS OF DENVER AND MOUNTAIN PARKS, Colo. Mus. Nat. Hist., Denver, Colo., 1939

Packard, F. M., BIRDS OF ROCKY MT. NAT. PARK, Rocky Mt. Nature Assn., Estes Park, Colo., 1950

Peterson, R. T., FIELD GUIDE TO WESTERN BIRDS, Houghton, Boston, 1961

Pettingill, O. S., A GUIDE TO BIRD FINDING WEST OF THE MISSISSIPPI, Oxford Univ. Press, N.Y., 1953

Robbins, Bruun, Zim and Singer, BIRDS OF NORTH AMERICA, Golden Press, New York, 1966.

Zim and Gabrielson, BIRDS, Golden Press, New York, 1956

BIRDS OF ALPINE HEIGHTS

summer plumage

winter plumage

WHITE-TAILED PTARMIGAN (12–13 in.) is a small grouse that remains above timberline except in winter. Summer plumage brownish; white in winter. Builds nest on the ground beside boulders.

HORNED LARK (7–8 in.) has a conspicuous yellow-and-black face pattern. In flight, light breast contrasts with its black tail. "Horns" are raised only during courtship. Lays 3–4 eggs in a ground nest.

BROWN-CAPPED ROSY FINCH (6 in. lives above timberline in souther Rockies; winters in valleys. Eats insect and seeds. Gray-crowned Rosy Finch i common in the northern Rockies.

WATER PIPIT (6–7 in.) nests abov timberline; hunts for insects aroun melting snowbanks. Bobs tail con stantly. In mating season, male sing while soaring.

BIRDS OF FORESTS AND HIGH SLOPES

WILLIAMSON'S SAPSUCKER (9½ in.) hunts commonly in pine woods for tree insects. The striped female differs so sharply from the male, it was formerly considered a separate species. Nests in holes of trees.

BLUE GROUSE (18–21 in.) is dark bluish-gray above, slate-gray below. Female is smaller and more brownish. Courting male utters hollow "hooting" sound. One race lacks white across end of tail.

WESTERN FLYCATCHER (8–9 in.) is olive-brown with light-yellow underparts, white wing bars and eye ring. Catches insects on the wing in forests and clearings. Builds moss nest in rocks or trees.

GRAY JAY (11–13 in.) has white crown and dark-gray collar. Lives in high forests and is seldom seen flying in the open. Gray Jays, commonly seen around camps, are called "Camp Robbers" or "Whiskey-Jacks."

TOWNSEND'S SOLITAIRE (9 in.), a solitary thrush with a warbling song, is slate-gray with white eye ring, light wing bars and white outer tail feathers. Breeds throughout the Rockies.

CLARK'S NUTCRACKER (12–13 in.) is common in high meadows in summer. It has a gray body with white patches on wing and tail, and a loud harsh call. It will enter camps for food.

MOUNTAIN CHICKADEE (5½ in.) hunts insects in bark of trees. It has a black cap and throat and white eye stripe. The Black Capped Chickadee lacks white over the eye.

HERMIT THRUSH (7 in.) is a brown backed bird with reddish tail, slender bill and spotted breast. Feeds on insects. Has a clear, flute-like song. Note slow, frequent raising of the tail.

100

KILLDEER (9–11 in.) is an inland plover of mountain meadows and lake shores. Common in the West, especially in summer. Note white-bordered reddish tail and two black breast bands.

RUBY-CROWNED KINGLET (4 in.) is a tiny, olive-gray bird with inconspicuous red crown, pale wing bars and white eye-ring. Feeds on insects. Builds hanging nest of bark or moss.

AUDUBON'S WARBLER (5 in.) is a bird of the pine and fir forests. Behaves much like flycatchers, catching insects on the wing. Builds feather-lined, bulky nest of bark and needles.

CASSIN'S FINCH (6 in.) often nests in pine trees. Feeds on insects and seeds. Note male's red crown, breast and rump. Tail is deeply notched. Female is olive-gray, and streaked.

PINE GROSBEAK (9 in.) is largest Rocky Mt. finch. Male is rosy-red with black wings and tail. Female is brownish-gray, has two white wing bars. These seed-eaters nest in conifers.

SPOTTED SANDPIPER (7–8 in.) teeters as it walks along lake shores. It is the only spotted sandpiper of the region. Note the white eye line and white shoulder mark.

101

RED CROSSBILL (6 in.) bobs as it flies, uttering repeated "beeps." Feeds on seeds from evergreen cones. The White-winged Crossbill of the N. Rockies has two white wing bars.

GREEN-TAILED TOWHEE (7 in.) feeds and nests close to the ground. Note the small bill, long wings and tail, green back and rusty red crown. Lays 4 eggs, white with brown speckles.

GRAY-HEADED JUNCO (6 in.) with rusty back, gray sides, pale bill and white outer tail feathers; feeds and nests on ground. Both the White-winged and Oregon Junco also occur in the Rockies.

LINCOLN'S SPARROW (5½ in.) prefers dense thickets. Note the breast, finely streaked with black, crossed by brownish-yellow band. Song Sparrow has heavier streaks which meet in central dark spot.

WHITE-CROWNED SPARROW (6½ in.) prefers brushy meadows. Mottled brown back, pearly-gray breast and conspicuous white-striped black head. Song consists of several whistles followed by a trill.

BIRDS OF VALLEYS AND FOOTHILLS

PINE SISKIN (5 in.) lives in coniferous forests but is generally seen flying overhead in flocks. Note heavy, brown streaks, forked tail, yellow wing bars, and unique, buzzing, ascending cry.

BROAD-TAILED HUMMINGBIRD (4 in.) closely resembles the E. Ruby-throated. Builds minute nest of moss, lichens, plant down and cobwebs. Wings make a high, whirring sound.

BELTED KINGFISHER (11–14 in.) lives near water and dives for small fish. Tunnels into banks to build its nest. Has a big head with a ragged crest, and a loud, rattling call. Female has chestnut breast.

BLACK-BILLED MAGPIE (19 in.) has a long, tapering, iridescent tail, white underparts and white V on its black back. Often gathers in flocks on trees or shrubs near the water.

RED-SHAFTED FLICKER (13 in.) is a white-rumped, brown-backed woodpecker, commonly seen on the ground probing for ants. Note undulating flight. Females lack red "mustache" marks of male.

103

VIOLET-GREEN SWALLOW (5½ in.) is metallic violet and green above with two white patches at base of tail. Flies high over cliffs. Tree Swallow is steel blue above; white below.

WHITE-THROATED SWIFT (7 in.) is only swift with white throat and breast. It feeds on the wing, and flies rapidly. Found in foothills near precipitous rock walls.

STELLER'S JAY (13 in.) has a tall, black crest, deep-blue wings and tail. Eats seeds, insects and fruit, and is conspicuous at forest campsites. Has a variety of loud calls.

LEWIS WOODPECKER (11 in.) is the only woodpecker with a rose-colored belly. Feeds like a flycatcher; flies like a crow. Food includes insects, berries, fruit and acorns.

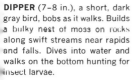

PYGMY NUTHATCH (4 in.) is often seen creeping head first down pine trunks, feeding on insects. Note its short tail. Usually travels in flocks, with a jerky bob-tailed flight.

DIPPER (7–8 in.), a short, dark gray bird, bobs as it walks. Builds a bulky nest of moss on rocks along swift streams near rapids and falls. Dives into water and walks on the bottom hunting for insect larvae.

CANON WREN (5½ in.) is reddish-brown with conspicuous white throat. Inhabits canyons and cliffs. Builds bulky nest in rocky crevices. Song is clear, rapidly descending whistles.

ROCK WREN (5–6 in.) is a gray-brown wren of rocky slopes with finely streaked breast and conspicuous white-tipped tail. Forages for insects. Lays 7–8 eggs in crevice nest.

Mountain Bluebird

Western Bluebird

female

male

BLUEBIRDS are common. The Mountain Bluebird (7 in.) is bright blue with a white belly; female is brownish. Western Bluebird (6½ in.) has rusty red back and breast; female is paler.

BREWER'S BLACKBIRD (9 in.) commonly walks with its wings slightly drooped. Feeds almost entirely on ground. Nests in colonies in grassy meadows. Its note is a rough "check." In the field, note the purple iridescence on the head and the white eye. Also common on the High Plains and eastward.

MACGILLIVRAY'S WARBLER (5 in.) recognized by its gray hood and white eye-ring, prefers moist hillside thickets; is often found near water. It lays 3–5 eggs in a nest of dried grass.

WESTERN TANAGER (7 in.) is brilliant yellow with black wings and a red face. Female is olive-green above, yellow below. Builds a twig-and-grass nest in pine, spruce or fir, fairly close to the ground.

BLACK-HEADED GROSBEAK (7 in.) nests in open, deciduous woodlands; feeds on insects and seeds. Note black head, heavy beak, rusty breast and white wing patches.

EVENING GROSBEAK (8 in.) is a large, dull-yellow finch with a whitish, conical bill and white wing patches. Easy to recognize. Eats a variety of seeds and fruits. Lays 3 to 4 eggs in a nest of roots and sticks.

LAZULI BUNTING (5½ in.) is a bright-blue finch with a cinnamon breast band and white wing bars. Female is dull brown. Prefers dry brushy slopes and hillsides. Nests in bushes.

RUFOUS-SIDED TOWHEE (8 in.) is a shy bird that nests and feeds in thickets or among dead leaves. Note the black head, reddish sides, white wing markings and white-tipped tail feathers. The western form of this common bird (illustrated) has many white spots on wings and back. Female smaller and browner. A summer resident in most of the Rockies.

107

ROCKY MOUNTAIN FISHES

Famed for trout in its swift, cold streams, the Rockies also have scores of other fishes, some preferring the larger lakes and rivers. Still other species, including Mississippi Basin forms, occur in foothill rivers and ponds. Typical fishes of the Rockies are illustrated here. See also FISHES, Zim and Shoemaker, Golden Press, N.Y., 1956. Remember that a state license is required even for fishing in National Parks, Monuments and Forests.

TROUT are the region's number one fresh-water game fish. Best known is the Rainbow or Steelhead, with a clear, reddish band along its sides. Rainbows feed on insects, small water animals, and fishes. Av. wt. 2–5 lb. Record 37 lb. The Cutthroat is silvery gray, deeply spotted with black. Note the red streaks on lower jaw. Wt. 1–3 lb.; record 41 lb. The Eastern Brook Trout has been introduced. It is dark olive, with "marbled" black and red spots along its sides. European Brown Trout, also introduced and fairly common, is dark above, silvery below, with numerous large black spots. A rapid grower; weighs 1–5 lb.; record 39 pounds.

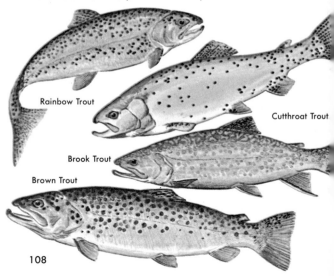

Rainbow Trout

Cutthroat Trout

Brook Trout

Brown Trout

MONTANA GRAYLING is similar to trout, but related to whitefish. It is an iridescent, purplish-gray, with a very large dorsal fin. Prefers cold streams. This popular game fish grows to 15 in. or more.

SQUAWFISH, the largest native minnow, is said to reach a weight exceeding 30 lbs., though 2–5 lbs. is average. An excellent sport fish on light tackle with bait or lures but are too bony to be good eating.

ROCKY MOUNTAIN WHITEFISH is found in lakes and streams on both slopes of the Rockies. Bluish above, silvery below; head rounded, overhanging snout; fins with black tips. Weight 1–3 pounds.

NORTHERN SUCKER has a long snout and fine scales. Males have wide, reddish streaks in spawning season. Suckers are tasty fish, caught in clear streams and commercially in lakes. Length, 15–18 in.

ROCKY MOUNTAIN REPTILES

The general environment of the Rockies does not meet the requirements of reptiles too well. These interesting vertebrates occur, but not in great number or in wide variety. Those concerned about snakes will be glad to know

WESTERN SKINKS are shy, swift, fine-scaled lizards with a tail longer than their body. Two species, one with light stripes; the other with dark. Length, 8–9 in.

FENCE LIZARDS with coarse, spiny scales are dull, gray-brown with dark and light blotches. Several species occur in the Rockies, living in dry, wooded areas or in rocky areas. Length, 5–7 in.

SHORT-HORNED LIZARD (3–5 in.) is a flattened, short-tailed lizard with a spiny head crest. Prefers dry, rough terrain. Easily caught, but not a good pet. Wrongly called "Horned-toad."

PAINTED TURTLE, common in the East, also occurs in northern Rockies. This western subspecies has less color on the sides and a large, regular, dusky patch on the lower shell. 7½–10 in.

he region supports just one average-sized species of rattler—the only poisonous reptile in our area. In all, the region has about 14 species of snakes, seven of lizards and four kinds of turtles. For further information read AMPHIBIANS AND REPTILES OF WESTERN NORTH AMERICA, Stebbins, McGraw-Hill, N.Y., 1954.

RACER The western forms of the common racer are thin, active snakes that feed on small animals. They are olive, bluish or brownish above, and yellowish below.

WESTERN GARTER SNAKE occurs in several forms. The Gray Garter Snake (illustrated) prefers dry places. Greenish gray to brown with a broken yellow stripe and black blotches on sides.

GOPHER SNAKE, a smaller western form of the Bull Snake, has dark blotches on the back joining those on the sides. They feed mainly on rats and other rodents, and hiss violently when molested.

WESTERN RATTLESNAKE, a medium-sized, thick-bodied species (3–4 ft.), is gray, greenish or brown with large irregular black spots. It has a triangular head. Feeds mainly on rodents. Poisonous.

111

ROCKY MOUNTAIN AMPHIBIANS

WESTERN TOAD (3–5 in.) is warty, gray, brown or greenish. Belly and chest speckled with black. Active at night at all but highest elevations. Males have chirping, bird-like call.

SPADEFOOT TOADS, 1½–2½ in., (three species) are more common in lower altitude grasslands and open areas. Note rounded, sharp-edged black bump or "spade" on feet, and vertical pupil of eye.

LEOPARD FROG (3–4 in.), the widest ranging North American amphibian is in all waters of the area, in both mountains and lowlands. Greenish, brownish or gray with oval or round black spots.

SWAMP CHORUS FROG is a smaller (1½ in.) frog of moist grasslands and streamside brush. Gray-green to olive brown, with five irregular dark stripes. Its call is a short chirp.

TIGER SALAMANDERS are blackish with variable light colored markings. They live in burrows in moist ground or under logs and stones and in water during the breeding season. Active at night.

ROCKY MOUNTAIN INSECTS

With the great variation in altitude, temperature, moisture, and character of the land, it is no wonder that the Rockies are rich in insects. Southern species enter this area from Mexico and the Southwest; eastern and Plains species push up into the foothills; and northern forms come south at high altitudes. Colorado boasts of more species of butterflies than such climate-favored states as California and Florida. Watch for those illustrated and many others. For sizes, approximate wing spreads are given in inches.

COLORADO ARCTIC (1.6 in.) prefers high altitudes, usually flying above the timberline. The larva feeds on sedges. The adult is a dull, brownish-gray; females are possibly more tannish.

MAGDALENA ALPINE (1.9 in.) is an unusual, velvety-black butterfly of the alpine zone. Occasionally large broods appear, but the life history of this collector's item is unknown.

OCHRE RINGLET, (1.2–1.8 in.) abundant and easy to recognize by its yellowish-brown color; often has a dark spot on each forewing and smaller spots along the edges of the back. New Mexico northward.

COLORADO HAIRSTREAK (1.5 in.) is the largest member of a group of small but beautiful butterflies. Found at lower altitudes in scrub and open woods. The larva feeds on scrub oak.

EDWARDS' FRITILLARY (2.5 in.) has heavy black borders with olive-brown undersides. Frequents open forests and grasslands. Females often feed on roadside thistles. Range: S. Canada to Colorado and Nebraska.

COLORADO ANGLEWING (2.0 in.) i found along wooded mountain stream and valleys from Idaho and Wyoming south to New Mexico. Wing border ragged; undersides with varying pat terns of gray.

COLORADO MARBLE (1.7–2.0 in.) is common from the lowland meadow to timberline forests. The pale-green larvae feed on plants of the mustard family. Found in the Rocky Mts. north to British Columbia.

larva

ALEXANDRA'S SULPHUR (1.9–2.3 in.) is common above 6,000 feet. Undersides of hind wing are pale grayish-green. Female pale yellow or white; lacks conspicuous black borders. Larvae eat legumes.

WEIDEMEYER'S ADMIRAL (2.1–2.6 in.) inhabits moist meadows, valleys, foothills and mountainsides. Larvae feed on cottonwood; hibernate in rolled-up leaves. Found from N. Mex. north to Montana.

MOURNING CLOAK, (2.8–3.2 in.) a widespread North American species, has purple-brown wings with blue-spotted yellow borders above, dark undersides. Caterpillars feed on soft-leaved trees.

PARNASSIAN (2.3 in.) is seen near stonecrop in forest openings, fields and open grasslands. High and low altitude forms vary in size. Weak fliers. Range: northern N. Mex. to southern Canada.

WESTERN TIGER SWALLOWTAIL (3.3–4.3 in.), commonest of several large swallowtails. Larvae feed on willow, cottonwood and aspen. Common from Plains westward, New Mexico to Alaska.

larva

larva

It would take a lifetime to see and learn to know the Rockies, but even a short vacation makes a beginning. Here are some places to go and the kinds of things to see, enjoy and understand in the Rocky Mountains.

Tour through National Parks and Monuments which preserve the best of our country's natural and historical heritage.

Take short side trips or camping trips to state and provincial parks and National Forests.

See birds, game, and other wildlife in their natural habitats; observe alpine plants, rocks and geologic formations; watch bubbling mud pots and erupting geysers.

Boat on mountain-ringed lakes or take guided trips down swift, white-water rivers, through colorful canyons.

Visit historic sites, Indian reservations, battlefields, ghost towns, museums and exhibits.

Walk the nature trails at leisure; hike the valleys, woods or the mountains on marked trails. Take pack trips by horseback, or try the challenge of mountain climbs.

Rest and relax at campgrounds shaded by tall pines, in resort hotels, at informal dude ranches, or at well-equipped cabins.

Try winter sports at ski centers or just enjoy the magnificent views from lifts, tows and elevated tramways.

Fish the unspoiled lakes and streams; hunt for game with gun or camera.

Sample rodeos, roundups, frontier days, fairs, and Indian ceremonials.

NATIONAL PARKS AND MONUMENTS (4 Parks and 6 Monuments) under the National Park Service preserve over four million acres of some of the most interesting parts of the Rocky Mountain region. Set aside by Congress or by presidential proclamation because of their unique value, these areas have ample facilities for visitors. Camping is usually permitted. Rangers and ranger-naturalists offer lectures and guided trips during the summer season. Larger Parks have museums. Check season dates and make reservations for lodging at peak travel times. Moderate entrance fees are charged by most Parks.

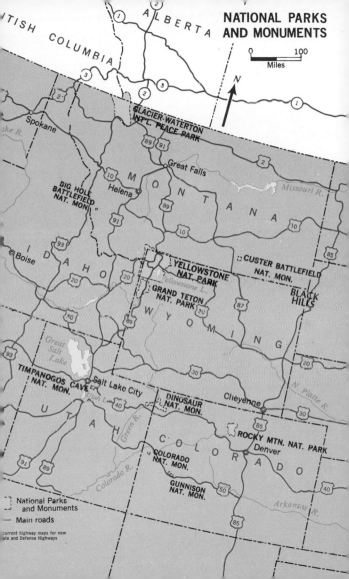

NATIONAL PARKS
AND MONUMENTS

0   100
Miles

N

BRITISH COLUMBIA

ALBERTA

Spokane

GLACIER-WATERTON
INT'L. PEACE PARK

Great Falls

M O N T A N A

Helena

Missouri R.

BIG HOLE
BATTLEFIELD
NAT. MON.

Boise

I D A H O

YELLOWSTONE
NAT. PARK

CUSTER BATTLEFIELD
NAT. MON.

BLACK
HILLS

Yellowstone L.

GRAND TETON
NAT. PARK

W Y O M I N G

Great
Salt
Lake

TIMPANOGOS CAVE
NAT. MON.

Salt Lake City

Utah L.

U T A H

DINOSAUR
NAT. MON.

Cheyenne

N. Platte R.

Green R.

ROCKY MTN. NAT. PARK

Denver

C O L O R A D O

COLORADO
NAT. MON.

Colorado R.

GUNNISON
NAT. MON.

Arkansas R.

National Parks
and Monuments

Main roads

current highway maps for new
ate and Defense Highways

Rare Trumpeter Swans nest along secluded lakes in Yellowstone

YELLOWSTONE NATIONAL PARK, oldest (1872) and best known National Park, is also the largest (2.2 million acres). It fills the northwest corner of Wyoming, running over into Montana and Idaho. Early reports by hunters and trappers of the natural wonders of the Yellowstone area seemed so fantastic that they were labeled fiction. Volcanic activity has created breath-taking scenery and is still evidenced in the largest collection of geyser basins in the world (300 geysers, large and small). Old Faithful, the most famous, erupts regularly, lofting some 10,000 gallons of water 140 feet into the air, at intervals of about 65 minutes.

Grand Loop Road, a 142-mile scenic highway, connects with the five main entrance roads and passes close to most of the major attractions in the Park. West, south and east entrances are open May 1 to November 1. The north entrance at Gardiner, Montana, is open all year and snowplows usually keep the route open through Mammoth Hot Springs, Tower Junction and Northeast Gate to Cooke. Hotels and inns close in mid-September. Many campgrounds are available in summer. Dude ranches surround the Park.

U.S. National Park Service
Old Faithful erupting

The Loop Road leads to hundreds of hot springs, bubbling mud pots, sinter cones, and terraces, often brightly colored by living algae. At Mammoth Hot Springs there are a museum and trails through the spring area. Also see Yellowstone Falls, the many-hued Yellowstone canyon, relics of a petrified forest, and a mountain of volcanic glass (obsidian).

More than 200 species of birds, including the rare Trumpeter Swan and White Pelican, are found in the Park. You may see moose, elk, bison, bighorn or mountain sheep, mule deer, antelope, black and grizzly bears, beavers, and coyotes. Lodgepole Pine and broad-leaved trees dominate the lower elevations; alpine wildflowers blossom in mid-summer near remnant snowbanks. Hear ranger-naturalist talks at museums and geyser basins.

Boiling mud pot

U.S. National Park Service

Do not feed the Bears

U.S. National Park Service

Longs Peak rises to 14,256 ft. behind Bear Lake, Rocky Mt. National Park

ROCKY MOUNTAIN NATIONAL PARK includes more than 60 glacial-cut peaks extending above 10,000 feet. Five lingering glaciers, U-shaped valleys, and many tarns or glacial lakes are reminders of the recent ice ages. Pink moss campions and yellow snow buttercups bloom in alpine meadows. Blue columbine and many other flowers are common at lower elevations. Mountain meadows, alpine tundra, and slopes of pine, fir, aspen, and spruce provide food and shelter for birds and small mammals. Here, too, are herds of elk, colonies of beaver, and bands of bighorn sheep.

Trail Ridge Road (open summers only), highest paved through-highway in the United States, with about ten miles above timberline, permits glimpses of several distinct communities of plant and animal life. At the western end is Grand Lake, largest high glacial lake in Colorado. Visit the museum and visitors center (Moraine Park) the alpine museum (Fall River Pass) and several self-guiding, nature trails.

Although evidence of glacial action is widespread throughout the Park, and snowbanks may persist all summer, the glaciers, magnificent from a distance, can be reached only by foot trails or by horseback trips. Experienced hikers may want to scale Longs Peak (14,256 ft.), McHenry Peak, or Mt. Richtofen (in the Never Summer Mountains). A guide is recommended. Get advice from a Park ranger. The Park is open all year, though some roads are closed in winter. The summer program includes talks, walks, movies, and motor caravans. Lodges, inns, and hotels operate near the Park along all nearby roads. Winter sports are popular at Hidden Valley on Trail Ridge but winter accommodations are more limited. Good campgrounds are numerous. The Park's eastern entrances are Fall River, near the valley village of Estes Park, and at nearby Thompson River; Grand Lake is the western entrance. Estes Park, with many stores, services, and tourist attractions, has an aerial tramway to the summit of Prospect Mountain.

Dream Lake lies near the foot of Hallet Peak, Rocky Mt. National Park

WATERTON-GLACIER INTERNATIONAL PEACE PARK on the Montana-Canada border includes Glacier National Park in the U.S., and adjoining Waterton Lakes National Park in Alberta. About 60 small glaciers still cling to the colorfully sculptured, sedimentary rock of high valleys and feed over 200 forest-edged lakes—some many miles in length. Finely ground and suspended sediment from the glaciers creates the varied colors in the lakes and the milky appearance of streams.

Snow may block high mountain passes from early fall to late spring, but hotels are open and tourist services available from June 15 to September 10. Going-To-The-Sun Highway links Lake McDonald and St. Mary Lake and offers a spectacular 50-mile crossing of the Continental Divide. Another road leads from Glacier National Park into the Waterton Lakes Park. Main scenic feature of the smaller, Canadian portion of the Park is the long ribbon of Waterton Lake which fills a rounded glacial carved valley. The lake is surrounded by conifer-clad slopes of snow-capped but glacierless peaks.

Grinnell Glacier (left) and Mountain Goat (right), Glacier National Park

U.S. National Park Service

U.S. National Park Service

A famous hotel overlooks Waterton Lake

In and around both Glacier and Waterton Parks, hotels, cabins and campgrounds are available in summer. Hiking and horseback trails radiate from the popular centers of Many Glacier and Two Medicine. There are over 1,000 miles of trails in Glacier National Park alone and many on the Canadian side, too. Ranger-naturalists provide guided trips and evening programs during summer months.

From spring to late summer, glacier lilies, beargrass, and blue gentians dot the mountain meadows. White Rocky Mountain goats can be sighted on distant cliffs. Bison, elk, deer and bears (black and grizzly) also roam the Park. This area was once the hunting ground of the Blackfoot Indians. See the Museum of the Plains Indian at Browning, 12 miles east of the East Glacier.

123

Visitors enjoy wild flowers near Jenny Lake; Tetons in background

GRAND TETON NATIONAL PARK (season June 15 to September 15) in northwestern Wyoming is dominated by jagged, glacial-cut peaks rising abruptly almost 7,000 ft. above the plains. Lacking foothills, the Tetons contrast sharply with the sage and grassland meadows of Jackson Hole, historic fur-trapper country to the east. Jenny Lake and other smaller glacial lakes flank the Teton front. Mountain climbers throng to the Tetons. Novices who want to scale the Grand Teton (13,766 ft.) can train at the Park-approved School of Mountaineering at Jenny Lake. Less ambitious visitors can enjoy the trees and flowers, the unique geology and glimpses of bison, moose, and elk. Visitor centers are located at Colter Bay, Jenny Lake, and Moose. Public campgrounds and other accommodations are available. A herd of more than 10,000 elk winters at Jackson Hole Wildlife Range.

he Canadian Rockies, averaging only about 70 miles
cross, extend northwest for hundreds of miles into
laska. Western Canadian National Parks are concen-
ated in southern Alberta and British Columbia. Many fine
rovincial parks, similar to U.S. state parks, are also found
this region. All parks of the Canadian Rockies, because
their proximity and similar climates, have similar flora,
una, and Alp-like scenery—mountains carved by glaciers
nd spotted with icefields, or with snow-capped peaks.

Chalets, hotels, cabins, and public campgrounds pro-
de accommodations for visitors. Resident park officers
re on duty to assist. Mountain climbing, hiking, boating,
nd fishing are popular. In season, try skiing, skating, and
ther winter sports. Make inquiries for winter trips and
ccommodations as part of the area is closed. See p. 138
r provincial parks.

National and provincial Canadian parks

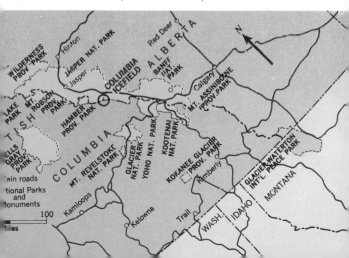

Lake Louise lies below a small glacier in Banff National Park

BANFF NATIONAL PARK, the first (1885) unit in Canada'
National Park system, includes snow-streaked, purple-gra
peaks, heavily wooded slopes, cascading waterfall:
verdant valleys, and trout-stocked lakes. At the south c
the Park (and best seen from the Calgary road, Rt. 1A),
spearheaded Mt. Assiniboine, the "Matterhorn of America
(11,870 ft.). North of Banff (main entrance and Par
headquarters), the Trans-Canada Highway leads to Britis
Columbia over Kicking Horse Pass or on to Lake Louis
in the Lakes of the Clouds district, most popular wilde
ness spot in Canada. The surface of this deep (over 20
feet), clear, opalescent-green lake, walled off from rufflir
breezes, provides a perpetual reflection of Mt. Victori
Glaciers and ice fields increasingly dot the chiseled pea
toward the north, terminating on the Banff-Jasper bord
in the 100-square-mile Columbia Icefield.

JASPER NATIONAL PARK, north of Banff, includes more of the extensive Columbia Icefield, out of which juts Snow Dome, the hydrographic center of the North American continent. The Athabaska River, bound for the Arctic Ocean, rises here and water also flows into streams that empty into the Atlantic and Pacific. Athabaska Glacier is accessible to visitors by foot or by snowmobile. Many more glaciers and Mount Columbia (12,294 feet), highest point in Alberta, are in this Park area. Largest of the many lakes is Maligne, nestled in an Alp-like setting. Other points of interest include Mt. Edith Cavell with nearby Angel Glacier, shaped like an angel with outspread wings, and Miette Hot Springs pool. Jasper Park harbors such wild animals as the wolverine, wolf, otter, grizzly, bighorn sheep and Rocky Mountain goats. Jasper, a year-round resort center on Jasper Lake, can be reached by road from Banff, by rail and road from Edmonton on the east, and from British Columbia over Yellowhead Pass.

Drainage from Columbia Icefield flows in three directions

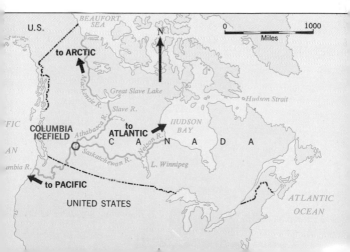

YOHO NATIONAL PARK, over Kicking Horse Pass from Banff, is rugged, glaciated, mountain country where the Yoho River, fed by the Wapta Icefield, flows through scenic Yoho Valley. Worth seeing also are fossil deposits, 1,650-foot Takakkaw Falls, many glacial lakes and alpine wildflowers in summer. Kootenay Nat. Park adjoins to the south. Highlights here are Marble Canyon and Radium Hot Springs.

GLACIER AND MT. REVELSTOKE NATIONAL PARKS lie in the Selkirk Mountains west of the main Rockies. Both contain a mixture of Rocky Mountain and Pacific Northwest flora, especially evident in the forest trees. Wildlife is abundant amid glaciated mountain scenery. Glacier, a climber's paradise, and Revelstoke, a center for winter sports, can be reached by rail and highway.

Snowmobile, Columbia Icefield, Jasper National Park

National Parks Branch, Dept. of Northern Affairs and National Resources, Ottawa

Partly cleared bones in the famous Dinosaur Quarry

DINOSAUR NATIONAL MONUMENT (northwestern Colorado and northeastern Utah) includes a world-famous dinosaur quarry and some of the most impressive wilderness canyon country in the West. Most accessible, and open all year, is the quarry north of Jensen, Utah, around which has been built a modern visitors' center. Here exhibits and ranger-naturalists interpret the story of the dinosaurs. Visitors may be able to watch workers clearing dinosaur bones in the tilted Morrison sandstone beds in the north wall of the museum. More than twenty excellent skeletons have already been removed.

Side roads lead to the uptilted, interior country, dissected by the Green and Yampa rivers into deep, red-to-white walled canyons and tree-dotted parklands, such as Echo Park, in the shadow of massive, sandstone Steamboat Rock. Guided boat trips on these rivers are available. Far above, semi-arid juniper and piñon forests edge the rimrock. Ancient Indian sites can be seen in Castle Park and other areas.

129

BLACK CANYON of the Gunnison, a National Monument in western Colorado, is one of the deepest, narrowest chasms in the world. The river has slowly cut through an uplifted block of hard crystalline rock. Take the road along the southern rim for a series of views.

COLORADO NATIONAL MONUMENT, 4 miles from Grand Junction, preserves a gem of wind and water erosion. Fluted columns of red sandstone and cliffs a thousand feet high vie with odd-shaped rock formations. Drive in No Thoroughfare Canyon. Use the campground. Open all year.

TIMPANOGOS CAVE is a National Monument on the slopes of the Wasatch Range near Salt Lake City. Stalactites, stalagmites and many branched helictites can be seen in the illuminated but chilly caverns. A scenic trail zig-zags over 1,000 feet up to the cave entrance.

BIG HOLE BATTLEFIELD, a National Monument, is the site southwest of Anaconda, Montana, where one of the last battles against the Indians was fought in 1877. Here U.S. troops engaged a large force of poorly-armed Nez Perce Indians under Chief Joseph, who was leading his band to safety in Canada. In the battle, 89 Indians were killed, over 30 of whom were women and children.

CUSTER BATTLEFIELD, southeast of Billings, Mont., is a National Monument that marks the site of the famous Battle of the Little Big Horn (below). Here General Custer, who had been warned of the large Indian forces, was killed and his troops were wiped out by the Sioux and Cheyenne under Sitting Bull and Crazy Horse.

Artist's interpretation of Custer's Last Stand

Highway Commission, South Dakota

Heads of four presidents are carved on Mount Rushmore

THE BLACK HILLS

Geologically like the Rockies, but a hundred miles east in South Dakota, is a great isolated rock island—the Black Hills. Rising several thousand feet above the surrounding prairie, the central granite core makes up most of the Black Hills skyline. This miniature version of the Rockies has its own distinctive attractions.

Some of the most imposing granite monoliths and spires of the Black Hills are included in Custer State Park and adjoining Norbeck Wildlife Preserve. In the center of this area is delightful Sylvan Lake. Custer State Park has a museum, a zoo and many recreational facilities. In addition to one of America's largest herd of bison, one can also see wild turkeys, bighorn sheep, and mountain goats (introduced). Needles Highway provides scenic panoramas. So does tunnel-spotted Iron Mountain Road to Mount Rushmore (above), site of Gutzon Borglum's 60-foot-high portrayals of Washington, Jefferson, Lincoln, and Theodore Roosevelt, carved on the face of the mountain.

South of Custer is Wind Cave National Park, open all year. Bison, antelope, deer and elk roam the area. To the west is another small but delightful cavern, Jewel Cave National Mon. East of the Black Hills lies the Badlands Nat. Mon., noted for its oddly eroded sediments and fossils of many mammals. Northwest some sixty miles is Devil's Tower Nat. Mon., a breathtaking, flat-topped volcanic plug, 1,280 ft. high, formed some 20 million years ago and now exposed by erosion. A museum explains the story of this unique mountain. See the famed mining towns of Lead and Deadwood. Homestake Mine, active since 1878, is open to visitors. Deadwood retains many of its old buildings and the graves of Wild Bill Hickock and Calamity Jane.

Granite spires along Needles Highway, Black Hills, South Dakota
Highway Commission, South Dakota

Lumbering in Gallatin National Forest, Montana

NATIONAL FORESTS under the U.S. Forest Service cover much of the Rockies, where, in five states, they have an area twice that of New York. These Forests are multi-purpose public lands used for lumbering, mining, grazing and watershed protection. They are equally important for recreation and offer many sites for camping and picnicking. Hunting, fishing, horseback riding, boating and chilly swimming are also available in these Forests. Information available from local headquarters. See p. 14.

NATIONAL FORESTS AND HEADQUARTERS

Colorado: *Arapaho,* Golden; *Gunnison,* Gunnison; *Pike,* Colorado Springs; *Roosevelt,* Fort Collins; *Routt,* Steamboat Springs; *San Isabel,* Pueblo; *Uncompahgre,* Delta; *White River,* Glenwood Springs

Idaho: *Challis,* Challis; *Clearwater,* Orofino; *Coeur d'Alene,* Coeur d'Alene; *Kaniksu,* Sandpoint; *St. Joe,* St. Maries; *Targhee,* St. Anthony

Montana: *Beaverhead,* Dillon; *Bitterroot,* Hamilton; *Deerlodge,* Butte; *Flathead,* Kalispell; *Gallatin,* Bozeman; *Helena,* Helena; *Kootenai,* Libby; *Lewis and Clark,* Great Falls; *Lolo,* Missoula

Utah: *Ashley,* Vernal; *Cache,* Logan; *Uinta,* Provo; *Wasatch,* Salt Lake City.

Wyoming: *Bighorn,* Sheridan; *Bridger,* Kemmerer; *Medicine Bow,* Laramie; *Shoshone,* Cody; *Teton,* Jackson

WILDERNESS AREAS have been set aside to preserve wild and primitive regions of National Forests. Of the 29 Wilderness Areas (each with over 100,000 acres) many are in or near the Rockies. Of smaller size (5,000 to 100,000 acres) are the Wild Areas. Both are controlled by the U.S. Forest Service. A few roads and truck trails are kept open for fire protection, but access to Wilderness Areas is by foot, on horse or by canoe. These are the areas for "roughing it." Try a pack trip with a guide. Check regional forestry headquarters (p. 14) and read *Handbook of Wilderness Travel,* by Wells, Harper Bros., 1956.

WILDERNESS AREAS   Wyoming: Bridger, Glacier, North Absoroka, South Absoroka, Stratified, Teton. **Montana:** Anaconda-Pintlar, Beartooth, Bob Marshall. **Montana and Idaho:** Selway-Bitterroot. **Idaho:** Sawtooth. **Utah:** High Uintas.

WILD AREAS   Colorado: Gore-Eagle Nest, Maroon-Snowmass, Rawah, Uncompahgre, Wild Elk-Eagle Nest. **Wyoming:** Cloud Peak, Popo Agie. **Montana:** Absoroka, Cabinet Mts., Gates of the Mountains, Mission Mt.

There are many other areas in the Rockies, primitive, isolated and uninhabited, that are not officially Wild or Wilderness Areas.

Sawtooth Wilderness Area south of Stanley, Idaho

Bob and Ira Spring

NATIONAL WILDLIFE REFUGES, of the U.S. Fish and Wildlife Service, are more numerous to the east than in the Rockies. Seven are in the area and more are nearby. Herds of big game, flocks of waterfowl and other wildlife may be seen, giving visitors an unexcelled opportunity for observation and photography. Animals are protected except during occasional supervised hunting seasons, and many breed in the refuge areas. Since hunting is prohibited in National Parks, these too serve as refuges.

Information is available from refuge managers and from the Fish and Wildlife Service, Washington 25, D.C. Also read *Seeing America's Wildlife in our National Refuges,* by Devereux Butcher, Houghton, 1956.

SOME NATIONAL WILDLIFE REFUGES IN THE ROCKIES
(Mainly for waterfowl unless otherwise noted)

Idaho: *Camas,* Jefferson Co.—also pronghorns; *Minidoka,* Blaine and Cassia Cos.

Montana: *Benton Lake,* Cascade and Chouteau Cos.; *Nat. Bison Range,* Sanders and Lake Cos.—bison, elk, deer, bighorn sheep; *Red Rock Lake,* Beaverhead Co.—including rare Trumpeter Swan. Montana also has several large refuges east on the Plains.

Utah: Famous *Bear River Refuge* (Box Elder Co.) is west of the Rockies.

Wyoming: *Nat. Elk Refuge,* Teton Co.—also includes a variety of big game, waterfowl and upland gamebirds; *Pathfinder,* Natrona and Carbon Cos.—also pronghorns.

Waterfowl and shorebirds feed at Bear River Refuge, Utah

Montana Highway Commission

ave formations in Lewis and Clark
avern Park, Montana

STATE PARKS are less known and hence may not be as crowded as National Parks. They are more common in Idaho and Montana. British Columbia boasts of fine, large provincial parks and Alberta has many small ones. There are fewer state areas in the southern Rockies. Colorado has only roadside parks at present. Most of the large Canadian parks lie along the Continental Divide and include rugged mountain scenery. State parks (and many county or local parks) include facilities for recreation, picnicking and camping. Campground guides (p. 141) often give details on these facilities and on charges, if any.

MONTANA   Lewis and Clark Cavern State Park (entrance fee; guided tours) includes the third largest cave in U.S., 300 ft. deep with columns, spires and helictites. **WYOMING**   Hot Springs State Park near Thermopolis has four big and many small mineral hot springs, including one of the largest and hottest in the world. Indoor and outdoor swimming pools; elk and bison herds. **IDAHO** Heyburn State Park, at the southern tip of Coeur d'Alene Lake, includes streams and mountain foot trails. Lava Hot Springs Plunge southeast of Pocatello is a health center. **BRITISH COLUMBIA** has the largest provincial parks in the Canadian Rockies. Hamber, Mt. Robson, Wells Gray and Kokanee Glacier parks have much to offer in scenery, recreation and camping, as do many other smaller provincial parks. **ALBERTA** has over a dozen small parks in the western part and so has many roadside campgrounds. Check your road map.

FOR MORE INFORMATION write to agencies suggested on p. 14. Your inquiry will be forwarded if it cannot be answered directly.

Sunset in city park, Denver

DENVER rightly boasts of its unique system of some 49 parks, covering an area of 380 sq. miles. Most are in the mountains, forming a huge circle southwest of Denver. Some are within the city limits. The parks afford scenic mountain drives, views of many peaks, fertile valleys, watersheds, lakes, streams, and wildlife. Side trips over back roads, leading to ranches, mountain meadows and stands of pines and aspens, will prove rewarding, too. Most parks have picnic areas; some have museums.

Only 30 minutes west of Denver is Lookout Park and Buffalo Bill's Grave. Park of the Red Rocks, 14 miles west of Denver, contains the famous Red Rocks Theater, built into the natural Triassic red sandstone hogbacks. Here erosion has formed an acoustically perfect auditorium. A 30-mile trip to Bergen Park leads from Idaho Springs over Squaw Pass to Echo Lake and Summit Lake parks and over the highest auto road in the United States, to the top of Mt. Evans—14,260 feet. Here, in addition to the superb views, is a major cosmic ray laboratory. In Genesee Park, 20 miles west of Denver, and at Daniels Park, 21 miles south, bison, elk and antelope graze peacefully.

COLORADO SPRINGS is long famed as a resort area with a noted city park system. Nearby is the Garden of the Gods, a park of upturned, red sediments, including a huge balancing rock. A circle road tour gives a one-day view of the mountains. Other drives include the scenic Rampart Range Road and the Gold Camp Road. Best known attraction is Pikes Peak (14,110 ft.), reached by car via toll road or by cog railroad. Cheyenne Mt. Zoo and Will Rogers Memorial, Seven Falls and Cave of the Winds are also worth a visit. See Colorado College, the nearby Fine Arts Center, Pioneer Museum, and NORAD. About 7 miles north is the U.S. Air Force Academy. Grounds open daily; parades on Saturdays.

Pikes Peak from the Garden of the Gods, Colorado Springs

Josef Muench

Trail to Hole-in-the-Wall Camp, Glacier National Park

HIKING is rewarding. No maps are needed for the popular, well-marked trails. Farther afield the hiker should use the local U.S.G.S. topographical maps (p. 14). Visitors can try everything from easy nature walks to long wilderness trips with a guide. Don't overestimate your ability. High-country hiking is exhilarating but the "thin" air is tiring to newcomers. Hike with a companion. Stay on the trails and avoid short cuts. Suit your clothing and equipment to your trip. Comfortable shoes, warm clothing, plus a windbreaker are recommended. Take a slicker for summer showers. Leave word about where you are going and when you expect to return.

If your stay is long, inquire about local hiking clubs. The Sky Line Trail Hikers and the Canadian Youth Hostelers have annual excursions in the northern Rockies. Hikers can be easily tempted by mountain climbing (p. 142), which is at its best here.

CAMPGROUNDS are plentiful. Roadside picnic areas are common and increasing in number. Facilities at designated campsites range from crude clearings in Wilderness Areas to well-planned camps with cabins, tent platforms or trailer sites, tables, fireplaces, water, and restrooms. Some state parks charge small fees. Since campgrounds may be crowded from Memorial Day to Labor Day, plan to arrive at a campsite early. Lengths of stay are limited in the more popular campgrounds. Inquire in advance. Check at National Forest and Park headquarters for location of camps and maps, or use the guides listed below.

Campground Atlas of the U.S. and Canada, Bier and Raup, Alpine, 1960.
Campground Guide, Rand McNally.
Guide to Campsites, Camping Family, Inc., Hammond, 1961.
Intermountain West (Campsite Finder Vol. 3), Hartesveldt, Naturegraph, 1957.
Sunset Nature Campsite Directory, Lane, 1962.

Camping on Mirror Lake near Devil's Peak, Idaho

Bob and Ira Spring

MOUNTAIN CLIMBING

comes naturally in this land of "shining mountains." Colorado boasts of 54 peaks higher than 14,000 feet. No other Rocky Mountain state has any this high. Longs Peak, 14,255 ft., is a Colorado favorite. Mountain climbing takes an essential know-how which the inexperienced but physically fit visitor can acquire easily. For the novice, the only requirement is to keep on the trail. For difficult climbs a guide and full equipment are imperative. Beginners might try the basic instruction given every summer in Grand Teton National Park. Inquire locally for details of classes and guided climbs.

Bob and Ira Spring

Climbing Longs Peak, Colorado

Never start on a climb that will take you off marked trails without proper equipment and without first checking maps, trail details, and telling a friend or a Park ranger where you are going.

High Rocky peaks in Colorado include Mt. Elbert, 14,431, Mt. Massive, 14,418, and Pikes Peak, 14,110. Highest peaks in Wyoming are Mt. Gannett, 13,785 and Grand Teton, 13,766. Utah's King's Peak, 13,498, Montana's Granite Peak, 12,850, and British Columbia's Mt. Robson, 12,972, are other high mountains. Some of the best, and most difficult, mountains for climbing are not the highest ones.

GHOST TOWNS of the Rockies come from a century of mining booms. Some are neglected collections of crumbling cabins, but many are restored because of new mining activity or have become resorts and vacation centers.

Colorado: *Aspen* boomed in the 1890's; *Central City-Black Hawk*, once "richest square mile on earth," famous now for its old mining flavor; *Cripple Creek*, fifth richest gold center of world; *Leadville*, nation's silver capital around 1878; *Silverton*, center of San Juan mining district. Nearby are *Telluride, Ouray* and *Creede*. Also see *Waldorf*, one of region's highest ghosts; well-preserved *St. Elmo; Georgetown*, famous for its 14-curve narrow-gauge Loop. **Idaho:** *Idaho City*, once a territory capital; *Florence*, state's richest gold camp; *Pierce*, gold first discovered in 1860, and nearby *Yellowpine; Silver City*, most picturesque gold and silver ghost; *Bonanza*, and *Custer*, boom towns of the 1870's, also *Gem*, in the Coeur d'Alene area. **Montana:** *Bannock*, Montana's first capital; *Cooke*, old gold and silver town; *Gold Creek*, gold first discovered here; *Marysville*, one-time leading gold producer; *Virginia City*, Montana's second capital. **Utah:** *Alta*, once a bustling mining town; *Park City*, mines once yielded over $300 million; *Brigham Canyon*, began as a gold town; now copper; *Silver Reef*, now in ruins. **Wyoming:** *Bald City*, a short-lived gold camp; *Carbon*, first coal mining town; *Grand Encampment*, in the copper field, and *Dillon* with its tall outhouses; *South Pass City* and *Atlantic City* on the Continental Divide. **British Columbia:** Kootenay Lake country has mining ghost towns.

Leadville, Colorado was once the "silver capital"

Josef Muench

Half Moon Lake in the Wind River Range, Wyoming, in autumn

RIVERS AND LAKES (natural and reservoirs) are common in the Rocky Mountains, often serving a multiple use. They provide water for irrigation, power and drinking, aid in flood and erosion control, and make possible fishing, swimming, boating, water-skiing, and waterfowl hunting. Many lakes are man-made. All add a pleasing variety to the countryside. The real gems are the many small, glacial lakes, most of them off the beaten path. Thousands of small streams and the headwaters of many major rivers flow from the Rockies. Fishing is famous (p. 146). Inquire locally for boat trips on the larger rivers and lakes. Among the region's foremost lakes are:

Colorado: Grand, Shadow Mountain, Granby, Taylor Park, Trapper's, Maroon.

Wyoming: Yellowstone, Jackson, Cooper, Wheatland, Pathfinder, Seminoe, Boysen.

Idaho: Pend Oreille (Idaho's largest), American Falls, Palisades, Coeur d'Alene, Priest, Cascade, Big Payette, Walcott, Redfish, Island Park, Arrowhead, Blackfoot River.

Montana: Flathead, Hungry Horse, Holter, Hebgen, Tiber, Canyon Ferry, Georgetown, Wade.

Utah: Great Salt Lake (1500 sq. miles, very salty), Utah, Bear, Strawberry.

Alberta: Maligne, Louise, Kananaskis, Spray.

British Columbia: Kootenay, Arrow Lakes, Shuswap, Jewel.

SPRINGS, cold and hot, flow by the thousands. Those in contact with heated volcanic rock are hot. Largest concentration of hot springs (some 3,000) is in Yellowstone amid scenic geysers and mud pots. Other hot springs are the sites of pools and resorts. Better known spring areas are:

Colorado: *Canon City,* two sulphur springs, discovered by Pike in 1806; *Glenwood Springs,* Yampah Spring supplies largest (1,650 ft.) outdoor mineral pool in world; *Hot Sulphur Springs,* more than a dozen hot springs; *Idaho Springs* spa dates back to 1868; *Manitou Springs* with famous Soda Springs; *Ouray,* highest mineral springs and pool; *Pagosa Springs,* 153° springs heat homes; *Poncha Springs,* about 100 springs, up to 185°; *Steamboat Springs,* 157 springs and pools of various temperatures.

Idaho: Lava Hot Springs (state park), 140° mineralized water; Soda Springs (on Oregon Trail), variety of hot and cold springs; Malta, American Legion health plunge; *Hot Springs* (near Payette), hot medicinal water and mud baths; *Big Springs,* source of the North Fork of the Snake.

Montana: *Giant Springs* (near Great Falls), one of world's largest, 152°; *Mont Aqua,* mineralized water is bottled; *White Sulphur Springs,* resort.

Utah: Blue, Sweet Water, and Iron—all small springs.

Wyoming: Saratoga, a state reserve, medicinal waters; Thermopolis State Park, hundreds of mineral hot springs including largest in the world; Warm Springs, the 70° water once used by Oregon Trail travelers.

Alberta: *Banff,* Hot Sulphur Springs; *Jasper,* Miette Hot Springs.

British Columbia: Fairmont Hot Springs, one of sources of water for Columbia River; *Halcyon,* Radium Hot Springs, in Kootenay N.P.

Mammoth Hot Springs are the largest in Yellowstone National Park

Fishing Swift Current River, Glacier National Park, Montana

FISHING for trout is popular throughout the Rockies from New Mexico into Canada. Lakes and rivers are often stocked. Check locally for license requirements and catch limits. Visit the numerous fish hatcheries open to the public. Calgary, Canada, has world's largest trout hatchery.

WHERE TO FISH

Colorado: The Gunnison River, Conejos, Frying Pan and Colorado; Trapper's Lake and others. 15,000 miles of streams; 2,500 lakes.

Idaho: Buffalo River, Henry Lake, Payette Lake, Lake Pend Oreille, Priest Lake, Salmon River, Silver Creek, Snake River.

Montana: Big Hole River, Flathead Lake, Gallatin River, Georgetown Lake, Hebgen Lake, Madison River, Sun River, Tiber and Wade Lakes.

Utah: Duchesne River, Logan River, Provo River watershed, Strawberry Lake, Uinta Mountain streams, Utah Lake, Wanship Lake.

Wyoming: DeSmet Lake, Encampment River, Gros Ventre River, North Platte River, Pathfinder Lake, Seminoe Lake, Shoshone National Forest streams, Yellowstone River and Yellowstone Lake.

British Columbia: Brooks River, Clearwater River, Jewel Lake, the Kamloops and Kootenay Lake country, Kicking Horse River.

Alberta: Bow River and tributaries, the Kananaskis and Spray lakes, Oldman River headwaters.

HUNTING and trapping originally opened up the Rocky Mountain wilderness. The "old days" are gone but game is still abundant and many still come here to hunt. Elk and mule deer are prime fall game of the region. Less frequently bagged are grizzly and black bears, moose, bison, bighorn sheep, mountain goats and lions, white-tailed deer, and pronghorn antelope. Smaller game include bobcat, with trapping for beaver, skunk, muskrat, weasel and marten. There is good hunting for waterfowl along rivers and lakes. Upland gamebirds include sage hens, ring-necked pheasants, and several kinds of grouse. State licenses are required and can be purchased at most resorts and sporting goods stores. State game and fish departments at the state capitals offer hunting information. Finally, everyone can enjoy hunting with a camera. Excellent shots can be taken in parks where guns are prohibited.

Bison on National Bison Range near Dixon, Montana

Allan Cruickshank—National Audubon Society

MUSEUMS are plentiful in the Rockies, though Denver and Salt Lake are the only large cities. Most universities all the National Parks, and many National Monuments have natural history museums. There are good art museums, too. Local pioneer museums are popular. The geological exhibits in several local museums are worth taking time out to see.

Colorado: *Boulder,* Univ. of Colo. Mus.; *Canon City,* Mus. of Nat. Hist. *Colorado Springs,* Colo. College Mus., Fine Arts Center, Air Force Academy Mus., Ft. Carson Mus.; *Denver,* U.S. Mint, Mus. of Nat. Hist., Art Mus. Schleier Galleries, Clock Manor Mus. (clocks), Chappell Hse. (art), State Hist. Mus.—historical dioramas; *Golden,* Colo. School of Mines Geology Mus., Colo. Railroad Mus.; *Gunnison,* Western State College archeology mus.; *Montrose,* Ute Indian Mus. **Idaho:** *Boise,* State Capital Mus. (outstanding bird exhibits); *Pocatello,* State College Mus., Nat. Hist. Mus. **Montana:** *Billings,* Yellowstone Mus.; *Bozeman,* McGill Mus.; *Browning,* Mus. of Plains Indian; *Butte,* Montana School of Mines Geology Mus., Charles M. Russell Gallery and Mem. Mus.; *Helena,* Mont. State Mus. and Russell Gallery; *Missoula,* Art Mus. **Utah:** *Salt Lake City,* Latter Day Saints Church Mus. of Nat. Sci., State Capital Mus., Univ. of Utah art gallery and geology mus.; *Springville,* art gallery; *Vernal,* Utah Field Hse. of Nat. Hist. **Wyoming:** *Como Bluff,* "Creation" fossil mus.; *Cheyenne,* Wyo. Geology Mus. *Jackson Hole,* Jackson Hole Mus.; *Laramie,* Univ. of Wyo. Geology Mus. **Alberta:** *Banff,* Nat. Hist. Mus., Luxton Mus. (Indians).

Narrow gauge train in Colorado Railroad Museum

Herbert S. Zim

Polar Bears in the Denver Zoo

GARDENS, ZOOS and other exhibits are worth a stop. Plantings range from commercial iris crops at Boulder to rock and rose gardens and living study collections (arboretums). Zoos in the large cities are best. Avoid roadside zoos with a few caged animals, kept as tourist bait. Don't miss the self-guiding nature trails in National Parks.

Colorado: *Boulder*, commercial iris gardens; *Colorado Springs*, Cheyenne Mountain Zoo; *Denver*, Habitat Zoo and botanical gardens in City Park, Roseacre (roses, lilies, Japanese garden); *Grand Junction*, Lincoln Park Zoo; *Greeley*, Grasmere rock gardens; *Pueblo*, rose gardens in Mineral Palace Park, zoo. **Idaho:** *Caldwell*, municipal rose gardens; *Idaho Falls*, Sportman's Island Zoo; *Moscow*, Shattuck arboretum; *Payette*, Showberger botanical gardens; *Twin Falls*, Gaskill botanical garden. **Montana:** *Billings*, Wonderland Zoo; *Butte*, rock gardens; *Great Falls*, botanical gardens; Lions Park sunken gardens; *Red Lodge*, "See Em Alive" zoo. **Utah:** *Provo*, State fish hatchery and game farm; *Salt Lake City*, Liberty Park rose gardens and zoo, Hogle Gardens Zoo, International Peace Gardens, George Washington Memorial Grove. **Wyoming:** *Casper*, municipal gardens; *Cheyenne*, Great Plains horticultural station; Lions Park sunken gardens; *Lovell*, rose gardens; *Powell*, spring garden tours; *Thermopolis Hot Springs*, zoo. **Alberta:** *Banff*, Cascade Rock Gardens, buffalo paddocks; *Calgary*, Reader rock gardens (plants from around the world), Burns Memorial gardens, Brewery aquarium, fish hatchery, zoo

James R. Simon

Crow women in costume before a tipi

INDIAN RESERVATIONS are now self-governing centers of tribal life and industry—quite different from the heavily supervised camps of a century ago. Many tribes manage soil and water conservation. They run cooperative and civic projects. Visit those in and close to the Rocky Mountain area to see the progress made and the problems still ahead. Indians of today are farmers, cattlemen, and workers in many trades. Leather and beadwork are often for sale in community craft shops. Look for those bearing the seal of the Indian Arts and Crafts Guild. See also the Indian museums, showing life in the Rockies and adjoining High Plains before and during the period of exploration and settlement.

Colorado: So. Ute Res. and Ute Mountain Res. (Ute), south of our area. **Idaho:** Fort Hall Indian Res. (Shoshoni, Bannock) (Headquarters: Fort Hall, N. of Pocatello, Rt. 91.), Kutenai Res. (Kutenai). **Montana:** Blackfoot Agency & Res. (Blackfoot), Rt. 2, E. of Browning; Flathead Indian Res. (Flathead, Salish, Kutenai), N. of Missoula; Crow Agency & Res. (Crow Cheyenne), Rt. 87; Rocky Boy's Agency Res. (Cree, Chippewa), S. of Havre; Fort Belknap Res. (Assiniboin, Atsina), S. of Rt. 2; Fort Peck Agency & Res. (Assiniboin, Sioux), N. of Rt. 2. **Utah:** Uintah and Ouray Res. (Utes), S. of our area. **Wyoming:** Wind River Agency & Res. (Arapaho, Shoshoni), Rt. 287, N. of Lander. **Alberta:** Blood and Piegan Agency (Blood and Piegan); Stony Sarcee Agency (Assiniboin); Blackfoot Agency (Blackfoot); Sarcee Reserve (Sarsi).

HISTORICAL SITES in this region are mainly of local importance. Forts and trading posts were established during the first half of the 1800's. Then in the second half of the century came gold rushes, mining camps and boom towns. Recently old towns have been revived and rebuilt; forts have been restored or replicas constructed. See these landmarks of the not-so-distant past. Many include museums and exhibits. See those listed on p. 48.

State of Colorado

The restored Central City Opera House

Colorado: *Aspen*, silver mining town revived; *Central City*, restored, famous eller and opera houses; *Colo. Springs*, Pioneer Mus., historical coll.; *Cripple Creek*, mining town; *Denver*, Colo. State Hist. Mus.; *Fort Garland*, Kit Carson's dobe fort; *Georgetown*, silver mining, Hamill Hse.; *Greeley*, Meeker Mem. Mus.; *Leadville*, silver bonanza town, Healy Hse., Matchless Cabin; *Pueblo*, El Pueblo Hist. Mus.; *Sterling*, Overland Trail Mus.; *Trinidad*, Old Baca House. **Idaho:** Cataldo Mission, built 1842, off US 10, w. of Kellogg; *Ft. Hall*, trading and military post on Snake River west of present city. **Montana:** *annock* State Mon., former territorial capital, 25 mi. w. of Dillon, Big Hole attlefield Nat. Mon., 12 mi. w. of *Wisdom*, Rt. 43; *Billings*, Yellowstone Co. ist. Mus.; *Crow Agency*, Custer Battlefield Nat. Mon., mus., US 87, Owen State on., first settlement, off US 93, St. Mary's Mission nearby; *Helena*, Mont. tate Hist. Mus.; *Virginia City*, former territorial capital, mus., Rt. 34. **Utah:** *rovo*, Pioneer Mem. Bldg., exhibit; *Salt Lake City*, Pioneer Mem. Bldg., Main ., Pioneer Village Mus., Conner St., Utah Hist. Soc., Temple St. **Wyoming:** *ody*, Buffalo Bill Hist. Center and Mus.; *Ft. Bridger*, south of US 30S, original rt and army base, mus.; *Ft. Casper*, replica of old fort, mus., near *Casper*, Ft. aramie Nat. Mon., mus., 3 mi. s. of *Ft. Laramie*, Rt. 26, Independence Rock, med "register of the desert," Rt. 220, 50 mi. w. of Casper; *Lander*, grave of acajawea, n.w. off Rt. 287; *Laramie*, U. of Wyo., State historical collections nd archives.

FOSSILS abound in this, one of the world's richest fossi areas. However, don't expect to find dinosaurs lying along the roadside. Good fossils of vertebrates are hard to find difficult to extract and costly to prepare and mount. With luck one may find an occasional tooth or bone. Watch fo invertebrate and plant fossils, too. Visit local museums (p. 148). Try "rockhound" shops. Make local inquiries be fore hunting fossils. Deposits may be off paved roads and hard to locate without specific directions. Check also fo local guide books covering geology and mineral locations Best places for fossils are not in the Rockies proper but in "parks," foothills and adjoining High Plains where up turned or undisturbed sediments are exposed.

WHERE TO LOOK

Colorado: Eastern foothills, good collecting the entire length; *Canon City* dinosaurs and early fish; *DeBeque* (Devil's Playground), dinosaurs; *Morrison* dinosaurs and invertebrates; *Florissant,* fossil fish, many fossil plants and insects; *Pawnee Buttes,* fossil mammals including horses and camels; N.W and N.E. Colo., many fossil mammals—rhinoceros, mammoth, titanothere, saber toothed cat; good fossil exhibits at *Golden* (School of Mines). *Boulder,* Univ. o Colo. Mus., and *Denver* (Mus. of Nat. Hist.). **Idaho:** Petrified Forest (Sequoias in Malm Gulch near *Challis.* **Montana:** Near *Harlowton,* east of Helena, larg fossil beds with dinosaurs, mammals, turtles, lizards, crocodiles, birds, plants near *Conrad,* 70 miles north of *Great Falls,* many marine fossils in shal of Marias River tributary; dinosaur beds east of *Anaconda.* **Utah:** See Dinosau Quarry in Dinosaur Nat. Mon., exhibits of dinosaur bones in position; *Moun Timpanogos,* marine animals and plants in limestone; southwest of *Wasatcl* plant fossils in cliffs; *Price,* dinosaurs and titanotheres; *Logan,* seaweed; *Sa Lake City,* dinosaurs and other fossils on exhibit at University of Utah Geolog Museum; *Vernal,* outdoor life-size dinosaur replica, field museum. **Wyoming** Como Bluff west of *Laramie,* site of first Rocky Mountain dinosaur finds, man early mammals, and nearby "Creation Museum" contains many fossils; Poleca Bench north of *Cody,* fossil crocodiles and turtles; *Kemmerer,* one of greates fossil fish beds in world, together with fossil alligators, birds, plants; north c *Lusk,* limestone fossil beds containing some of best American Triceratop dinosaur remains; Black Hills, giant cycads (depleted), marine fossil-bearin shales at *Belle Fouche.* **Alberta:** Rich dinosaur beds—many localities for smalle fossils; *Calgary,* dinosaur gardens with replicas. **British Columbia:** *Field,* Bu gess shale deposits containing many early Cambrian marine fossils includin seaweeds, sponges, worms.

Smelter near Kellogg, Idaho—Coeur d'Alene mining district

ROCKS AND MINERALS made the Rockies famous. Min ing is still big business with a total production today greater than in the bonanza days of the late 1800's. Be sides gold and silver, the region is rich in molybdenum, vanadium, antimony, lead, zinc, copper and gem stones. Some operating mines are open to visitors and guided tours have been set up in abandoned mines. Visitors can pan for gold locally—good exercise. Check local guides on localities for mineral and gem collecting—they are legion. Some larger mining areas are listed below.

Colorado: *Climax*, molybdenum; *Gilman*, lead and zinc; *Idaho Springs-Central City* area and many others.

Idaho: *Kellogg*, heart of Coeur d'Alene mining district (lead, silver, gold and zinc); *Bunker Hill*, lead and silver; *Montpelier* area, phosphate deposits; *Wallace*, lead silver.

Montana: *Anaconda*, copper (Washoe Smelter); *Butte*, gold, silver, copper and zinc; *Helena*, gold, silver and lead.

Utah: *Bingham Canyon*, narrowest city in the world, has largest open-cut copper mine in the U.S.

Wyoming: *Greybull*, bentonite; *Kemmerer*, coal; *Rock Springs*, bituminous coal; *Gillette*, great strip coal mine.

British Columbia: *Kimberley*, summer tours through lead-zinc mine; *Trail*, large lead-zinc plant. Also widespread but small deposits of gold, silver, copper tin, cadmium, antimony and bismuth.

153

The Rockies offer magnificent views for the photographer—Boulder Peak, Glacier National Park

PHOTOGRAPHY in the Rockies can be disconcerting until visitors learn they tend to overexpose their pictures here. The higher one goes, the greater the light intensity. Unless your camera is automatic, or equipped with a light meter, close the shutter one stop more than what you would use for normal photographs back home. Snow cover calls for reduced exposure. Summer picture-taking time is best in the morning because of possible afternoon showers. Bad weather seldom lasts and the patient photographer will usually get his picture. Good lake reflections have to be caught early or late because of daytime breezes.

Color photography is best in the Rockies, but avoid strong light and shadow. Close-up lenses or extension tubes are essential for wildflower or other detail. A telephoto lens is helpful for birds, animals and in getting details of mountain scenery. Wildlife photography takes patience. Don't entice bears with food. It can be dangerous. Use a yellow or red filter with black and white film to give you contrast.

154

CULTURAL ACTIVITIES have become a feature of the Rockies, not only in the big cities, but also in the smaller mining towns which have been revived as centers of winter sport and summer recreation. Pageants, concerts, festivals and plays, including old-fashioned melodramas, make up the summer programs. Aspen, Colorado, is the oldest and most famous of these centers with a music and cultural program that has been going on for nearly twenty years. International artists participate just as they did in the boom days of the '90's. Check locally for schedules. Many colleges have summer courses in natural sciences with field work and week-end programs. Write them for catalogs.

Colorado: *Aspen,* Institute for Humanistic Studies, summer festivals, lectures, music and seminars. *Boulder,* U. of Colorado summer drama, concerts and lectures. *Canon City,* music blossom festival in May. *Central City,* summer performances at famous opera house during July. *Colorado Springs,* Garden of the Gods, summer concerts, Broadmoor International Center. *Cripple Creek,* old-time melodramas in summer. *Denver,* summer opera at Cheesman Park, concerts at Red Rock Park, summer theater at Elitch's Gardens. *La Junta,* Koshare Indian kiva and dances.

Montana: *Virginia City,* summer playhouse, 19th century drama.

Utah: *Salt Lake City,* Mormon Tabernacle Choir.

Wyoming: Summer pageants of the West at *Lander, Lusk* and *Daniel.*

Concerts are held in the huge Music Tent in Aspen

Atop Dollar Mountain, Sun Valley, Idaho

WINTER SPORTS are possible every month of the year in the snow-clad Rockies, but the "season" usually extends from December to May. Skiing is the top sport but lakes and rinks are available for ice-skating. Snowshoeing, bobsledding and tobogganing are done also. Ski tows are in operation at over a hundred sites from Sun Valley, Idaho, famous winter sports area, where there are several, to small, local lifts. Aspen, Colorado, a very much rejuvenated ghost town, has good ski slopes including four-mile Roch Run, one of the world's most difficult. Its 14,000-foot lift, rising 3,400 feet up Ajax Mountain, is one of the longest in the world.

OTHER ROCKY MOUNTAIN WINTER SPORTS AREAS INCLUDE:

Colorado: Arapahoe Basin, Berthoud Pass, Breckenridge, Broadmoor (closest to the Plains, augmented by artificial snow), Cooper Hill (Leadville), Crested Butte, Guenella Pass, Hidden Valley, Loveland Basin, Mesa Lakes (Grand Mesa), Monarch Pass, Pikes Peak, Pioneer (Gunnison), Red Mountain (Glenwood Springs), Redstone, Steamboat Springs, Winter Park.

Idaho: Island Park region, Magic Mountain (Twin Falls), Payette Forest (McCall), Pend Oreille region.

Montana: Big Mountain (Whitefish), Bozeman region, Butte region, Kalispell region, Red Lodge.

Utah: Alta, Beaver Mountain (Logan), Brighton, Snow Basin (Ogden).

Wyoming: Bighorn National Forest, Casper Mountain Park, Snow King Mountain (Jackson), Snowy Range (Laramie).

Alberta: Banff (Mount Norquay, Sunshine Lodge, Mount Temple Chalet, Mount Skoki Lodge), Jasper (Whistlers Mountain).

British Columbia: Mount Revelstoke, Red Mountain (Trail).

INDEX

Asterisks (*) denote pages on which the subjects are illustrated.

157